Using stories to teach

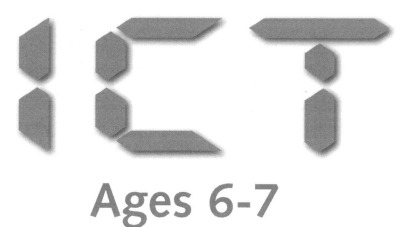

Ages 6-7

Anita Loughrey

Hopscotch

A division of MA Education Ltd

Hopscotch

A division of MA Education Ltd

Published by
Hopscotch, a division of MA
Education,
St Jude's Church, Dulwich Road,
London, SE24 0PB
www.hopscotchbooks.com
020 7738 5454

©2011 MA Education Ltd

Written by Anita Loughrey

Designed by Claire White,
Fonthill Creative, 01722 717029

Illustrated by Kerry Bailey

ISBN 978 1 90751 538 5

Contents

Introduction

ICT and the Primary Curriculum

Today children will arrive at school with an extensive knowledge of ICT and its capabilities. They have a knowledge and understanding that can sometimes be beyond some adults. The aim in school today is to harness their experiences and use them to enhance their learning in school.

ICT today is one of the best and fastest growing tools available for learning. It helps to:

- Make difficult and abstract concepts easier to explore
- Make learners partners in their formal learning
- Motivate learners and keep them engaged in learning
- Open up dialogue with parents and extend learning
- Personalise learning and give learners a voice
- Raise standards
- Reach the hard-to-reach
- Save you time and be more efficient.

In order for children to use and apply their ICT knowledge and understanding confidently and competently in their learning and everyday contexts, exciting and stimulating lessons must be provided.

ICT is no longer viewed as a separate curriculum subject but permeates all the other subjects. The children should be provided with stimulating activities that allow them to explore and become familiar with the technology resources available in the school, across a wide range of different subject areas.

About the series

The 'Using Stories to teach ICT' series of books demonstrates how ICT skills can be taught and extended whilst linking to a wide variety of other subject areas. There are four books in the series – two at Key Stage 1 and two at Key Stage 2.

They offer a structured approach with the non-specialist in mind and provide detailed lesson plans to teach specific ICT skills whilst linking to other areas of the curriculum. Each book contains ideas for communication, modelling, presentation, databases and control.

The aim is for ICT to be presented in a format that shows how information technology is used in our everyday lives. The imaginary situations portrayed in the stories act as a stimulus for the children's own investigations and creative work. The ideas in this series can be adapted to teach all areas of the curriculum.

Format of the books

Each book contains six stories that require the children to use and extend different ICT skills. Each story is accompanied by teachers' notes containing four separate lessons that can be used in conjunction with the story. Every lesson plan has a corresponding activity sheet.

The teachers' notes are broken down into the learning objective and the curriculum links with some suggestions for the type of hardware and software that will need to be made available. The activities have been sub-divided into:

- Resources – this is a list of what you will need to do the lesson
- Introduction – ideas to introduce the activities, with key questions and discussion points to reinforce the concepts and vocabulary required for the lesson
- Main activity – ideas for grouping and using the activity sheets
- Plenary – an opportunity to review and discuss the learning outcomes so children reflect on what they have learnt
- Extension – further ideas to extend their skills and technological knowledge.

The activity sheets can be found at the end of each chapter.

About the stories

The stories are designed to be a springboard to develop ICT within the classroom throughout a wide range of subjects due to the broad selection of cross-curricular links.

If possible enlarge copies of the story or project it on to a whiteboard so the children are able to see the illustrations and may be able to follow along as you read it aloud to the class. As the children get older and their vocabulary improves, encourage the children to read the stories aloud to each other.

There is a lot of scope for initiating a discussion about the wide range of technology used in our everyday lives and for extending from the given lesson ideas to your own ICT based projects.

Using the lesson plans

Within the planning we have added reference statements headed WALT, WILF and TIB as these or similar systems are often used to ensure lessons are focused, objective led and in context for the learner. They help summarise the purpose of the lesson, what is required of the children in order for them to successfully learn that lesson and why what they are learning is important.

 WALT stands for "We Are Learning Today"

 WILF stands for "What I'm Looking For"

TIB stands for "This Is Because"

Curriculum Overview

This chart gives an overview of the ICT covered by each story and the cross-curricular links covered by the activities over all four books in the *Using Story to Teach ICT* series. The relevant information for this book, aged 6-7, is shaded.

Book	Story	ICT	Cross-curricular link
Ages 5-6	Playground Proposal	Modelling	Design & Technology
	Football Crazy	Word Banks	Geography
	Song Quest	Presenting Information	Music
	The Cycle of Life	Labelling and Classifying	Science
	In the Garden	Pictograms	Mathematics
	How Does this Work?	Instructions	Literacy
Ages 6-7	The Pen Friend Diaries	Communicating Information	Literacy
	Celebrations	Communicate Ideas	RE
	Why do we Remember?	Finding Information	History
	Robot Postman	Routes	Geography
	Magic Carpet	Creating Pictures	Art
	Ice Cream Parlour Break-in	Questions and Answers	Mathematics/Science
Ages 7-9	School Play	Combining Text and Graphics	Literacy
	Jack and the Beanstalk	Manipulating Sound	Music
	Tiger Adventure	Databases	Geography/Mathematics
	It's Not Right!	Email	PSHE/Citizenship
	Mosaic	Repeating Patterns	Art/History
	Labyrinth	Simulations	Mathematics
Ages 9-11	Interior Designer	Graphical Modelling	Art
	Victorian Childhood	Complex Searches	Mathematics /History
	Surprise Party	Spreadsheets	Mathematics
	The Fairground	Control and Monitoring	Design & Technology
	Save the Polar Bear	Monitoring Environment	Literacy
	Security Alert	Multimedia Presentation	Design & Technology

The Pen Friend Diaries – teachers' notes

Learning Objective
To communicate information using text

Curriculum Links
Literacy

- Communicate with known audiences using ICT
- Gain a greater understanding of the keyboard in order to type accurately
- Use word processors to enhance the presentation of their writing.

It would be useful to link with another school or class before you undertake these activities so the children have a specific audience in mind for their letters and not an imaginary friend. Their letters could be sent by you as the teacher as attachments to an email, or printed and posted. Remember, the aim is to concentrate on word processing skills and not to teach them how to use email at this stage.

Activity One – Letters

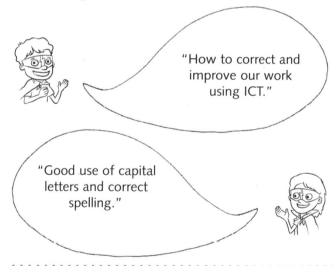

"How to correct and improve our work using ICT."

"Good use of capital letters and correct spelling."

Resources
- 'Letters' activity sheet
- 'Pen Friend Diaries' story
- Word Processing program such as Word
- Computers
- Printer
- Digital projector
- Interactive Whiteboard
- Scanner
- Link with another school or class
- Email facilities or envelope and stamp
- Laptop.

Introduction
Read the 'Pen Friend Diaries' story. Tell the children they are examples of letters created by older children using a word processor. Ask how it is different from handwritten work. Ask which is easier to read. Point out there is less likely to be any spelling mistakes.

Re-read the part of the letter where Robert explains to Josie that the teacher, Mrs Talbot, says he can check his spelling using the computer. How would they do this? Explain misspelt words will be underlined in red. Demonstrate how to check for spelling mistakes. Explain that, when they have changed the spelling, the corrections can not be seen. Show the class how to use the backspace and delete keys to correct mistakes as they type. Ask for volunteers to enter and correct text to reinforce how they check and change spelling mistakes.

Remind the children how to use the spacebar to create a space between words and how to use the shift key to make a capital letter. Identify where the return/enter key has been used to make new paragraphs in Robert's and Josie's letters.

Main Activity
Read the letters again. Identify what sort of things the two children tell each other. List their ideas.

Explain they are going to write their own letters to children in another school. Refer them to the list they made of things they could include in their letter. Try to include:

- Name
- Age
- The town, city or village they live in
- Things they are going to do that week
- What they would like to do in the future
- Things that have happened to them
- Things they have done recently.

Identify examples from the letters.

Tell them they are going to write their letters in rough first on the 'Letters' activity sheet. This will prevent them sitting in front of the computer and not knowing what to write. Remind them they can correct their work be using the delete and the backspace keys.

Remind the children to save a copy of their letters. They could also print out their letter and paste them onto another copy of the 'Letters' activity sheet.

Ask the children to print out their letters and suggest they make their own Pen Friend Diary containing a copy of their own letter and copies of the letters they are sent from the other school as a record of their communication.

Plenary

Project some of the children's letters on to the whiteboard. Point out good use of the spacebar and Capital letters. Remind the children they need to use a spacebar to make a space between words and they need to hold the shift key to make the letter a capital one. Ask which key they need to use to start a new paragraph. Reinforce it is the return/enter key.

Extension

Split the children into small groups and ask them to write a reply to Josie's last letter as if they were Robert. Use hot seating and other drama techniques to encourage the children to write in the role of Robert. When they have drafted their letters they could type up their replies in Word.

Activity Two – Word Processor Checklist

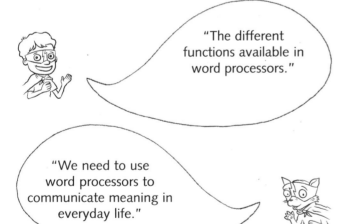

"The different functions available in word processors."

"We need to use word processors to communicate meaning in everyday life."

Resources

- 'Checklist' activity sheet
- 'Pen Friend Diaries' story
- Computers
- Digital projector
- Interactive Whiteboard
- Laptop
- Word processor like Word.

Introduction

Project one of the letters from the 'Pen Friend Diaries' onto the whiteboard. Discuss the presentation of the letter. Ask how they could change the way the letter looks.

Show the class the different functions available in word to enlarge text, make bold, italic and underline, change the colour, size and font style. Write a sentence and demonstrate these different functions. Ask for volunteers to make changes to a sentence on the screen. Ask the class what the child had to do to achieve this effect.

Main Activity

Ask the children to use the saved copy of their letter and change how it looks. Ask them to experiment using the different skills.

Tell the children when they have finished they should save the new letter under a different file name, using the 'Save as' function. Print a copy for display or to go in their own Pen Friend Dairy.

Plenary

Using the 'Checklist' activity sheet ask the children to work with a partner and discuss how to perform the different tasks. Encourage them to discuss with their partner what changes they made to the format of their letter and how they achieved this.

Ask them to explain what the specified keys on the keyboard do. Each child should then complete their own checklist as a record of what they can do.

Extension

Discuss how labels describe what things are. Ask the class to brainstorm in order to choose objects in the classroom that could be labelled. Ask the children to take it in turns to type a label in a suitably large font size that it can be seen from a distance. Ask them to correct any mistakes as they type using the delete and the backspace keys.

Activity Three
– Digital Cameras

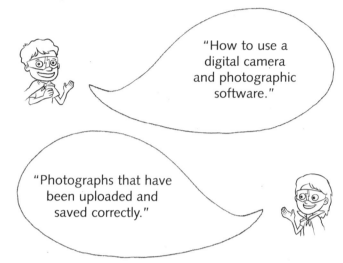

"How to use a digital camera and photographic software."

"Photographs that have been uploaded and saved correctly."

Resources

- Digital cameras
- 'Digital camera' activity sheet
- 'Pen Friend Diaries' story
- Connection lead
- Computer
- Printer
- Digital projector
- Interactive Whiteboard
- Scanner
- Laptop
- Photographic software such as Photoshop Elements
- Drawing program such as Paint.

Introduction

Read the 'Pen Friend Diaries' story to the class. Point out that Josie and Robert sent each other photos of themselves so they would know what each other looked like. Ask how would they have taken their photograph? Explain they would have probably used a digital camera but, take on other ideas, such as used a webcam photo shot.

Scan the 'Digital Camera' activity sheet into the computer and project onto an interactive whiteboard. Point out the different parts of the digital camera. Read the words in the word bank. Ask the children to identify the different parts of the camera and explain their function.

Ask for volunteers to come to the front of the class and label the camera using the word bank to help them. The children could then complete their own version of the 'Digital Camera' activity sheet. This could either be achieved by giving them a photocopy or loading the scanned version into a program such as Paint and letting them type their labels onto the screen.

Main Activity

Show the children how to take, upload and save a photograph on the computer.

Split the class into small groups of approximately four children and ask them to take a photograph of each person in their group. The children can then upload these photos into the computer, choose which one they like best and save it.

Demonstrate how to reduce the size of their photographs. Ask them to reduce the size of one of their photographs and save it with a different file name, using the 'Save as' function.

Plenary

Ask the children to print out a small, passport sized photograph of themselves. Ensure every child prints at least one photograph of themselves using the print function in the photographic software being used.

Stick their photograph onto card, laminate and use to label their pegs, desks or draws.

Extension

Some children may be able to add their photograph to their letter in Word before it is emailed or posted. Or if you prefer it could be printed separately and stapled to their letter to post.

Activity Four
– Speech Bubbles

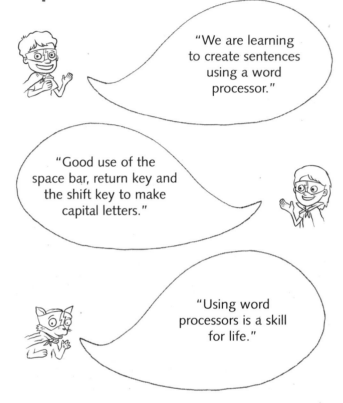

"We are learning to create sentences using a word processor."

"Good use of the space bar, return key and the shift key to make capital letters."

"Using word processors is a skill for life."

Main Activity

Split the class into pairs. Give each pair a copy of the 'Speech Bubbles' activity sheet. Ask the children to discuss what is being said. Remind them to use the space bar to create spaces between words and the shift key to make a capital letter.

The children could then either use a word processor to type the speech, print it and stick it onto photocopies of the activity sheet or you could load the 'Speech Bubbles' activity sheet into a drawing program software such as Paint and ask the children to type directly into the speech bubbles, save their work and print out a copy each.

Plenary

Ask for volunteers to share what they have written in the speech bubbles.

Extension

Ask the children to draw pictures and write their own speech bubbles of what Robert might say to Josie and vice versa if they ever met in person. This could be done using a drawing program such as Paint.

Resources
- 'Pen Friend Diaries' story
- 'Speech Bubbles' activity sheet
- Computer
- Printer
- Digital projector
- Interactive Whiteboard
- Laptop
- Scanner
- Drawing software such as Paint.

Introduction

Scan the 'Speech Bubbles' activity sheet into the computer and project onto an Interactive Whiteboard. Explain to the children the illustrations show a picture of Robert and his teacher Mrs Talbot. Discuss how speech bubbles can be used to illustrate direct speech.

Read the 'Pen Friend Diary' story to the class. Ask them what the teacher could be saying to Robert. What do you think Robert's reply might be?

Hello,

Mrs Talbot says I have to write you a letter, whether I like it or not, because we're going to be pen-friends.

I am seven years old and I like playing football, watching TV and playing on my X-box. What do you like doing?

When I leave school I am going to be an explorer and travel the world. At the moment I live in Croydon. I ride my bike to school every day. The roads here are very busy.

We have to type our letters out on the computer and print them out before we send them. Mrs Talbot says this is good because I can get the computer to fix all my spelling mistakes.

Next week we are going on a school trip to the South Wales for the day. I am really looking forward to it.

From Robert

Dear Robert,

Thank you for your letter. I hope you had a good time on your school trip to South Wales. We went on our school trip to the butterfly house.

I do not need to use the computer to help me with my spelling as I am the best speller in the class. I can spell really long words like imaginary and rhinoceros.

My school is in the Yorkshire Dales. I live on a farm. We keep pigs and chickens and I have my own horse called Daisy. I ride and groom Daisy every day. When I leave school I want to be a writer and also help on the farm.

Please can you send me a photo of yourself so I can see what you look like? This is a photo of me and my horse, Daisy.

Best wishes,
Josie

Hi Josie,

I told Mrs Talbot I didn't want to write to a girl but, she said I had to.

I like your horse. I have never been near a horse let alone ride one. I reckon it is very different from riding my bike. I haven't seen a real pig before either, except on the telly. There were lots of sheep in South Wales though. We could see them from the bus.

The school trip was brilliant. I had never been to the sea before. It was colder than I was expecting. I liked climbing on the rocks. Mrs Talbot got all stressed because she thought we were going to fall.

I have sent you a picture. That's me with a broken arm. I broke it on the bus on the way back from Wales. I was play-fighting with my best friend Jimmy.

The worst thing about breaking your arm is you are not allowed to play football at lunchtime. I wasn't even allowed to referee in case the ball hit me. The best thing about breaking your arm is you don't have to do any writing at school.

From Robert

Dear Robert,

Sorry I have not written for a long time. Our school was flooded after all the rain. We had a few days off school and then, the Council let us have some classrooms in our local secondary school. I was pleased about that because I missed seeing all my friends. Some people's homes were flooded too. Luckily, the farm was not affected.

They did a lot of rebuilding work in my classroom. Now we have new carpets, new computers, new cupboards and the walls have all been repainted light green.

I hope your arm is better. Was it very painful? I would not have liked not being able to write. It would have meant I would not be able to ride Daisy too. How did you ride your bike to school with a broken arm?

Next week, I am going to enter Daisy into the Great Yorkshire Show as the best groomed horse. Wish me luck.

Best wishes,
Josie

Hello Josie,

I couldn't ride my bike to school when my arm was broken in case I fell off and hurt it again, so I had to walk to school. Walking was Ok though. Me and Jimmy use to play this game to see what we could find in the street. One day, I collected four bottle tops, a comb, three elastic bands, a marble and 27p.

If my school was flooded it would be so cool. I wouldn't have to put up with Mrs Talbot moaning at my spelling all the time.

How did the horse thing go? Did you win?

From Robert

Letters

Name: _____

- Write or paste your letter here.

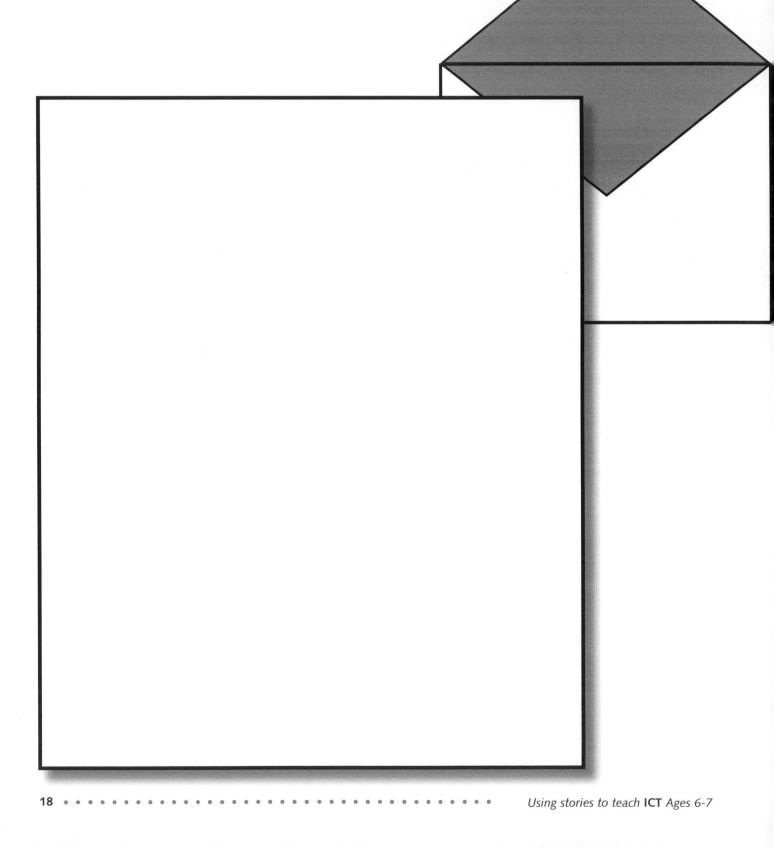

Using stories to teach **ICT** *Ages 6-7*

Name: _____

•   Tick the box to show what you can do on a Word Processor.

	I can make my writing bigger.
	I can make my writing smaller.
	I can make the letters bold.
	I can change the colour of my writing.
	I can change the font.
	I can make my writing italic.
	I can underline my writing.

•   Explain what these keys do:

Shift _____

Spacebar _____

Return/Enter _____

Insert _____

Backspace _____

Delete _____

Digital Camera

Name: _____

- Label the picture of the camera.
- Use the word bank to help you.

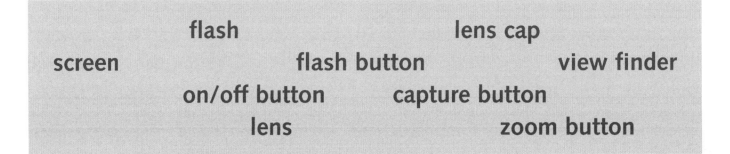

flash   lens cap

screen   flash button   view finder

on/off button   capture button

lens   zoom button

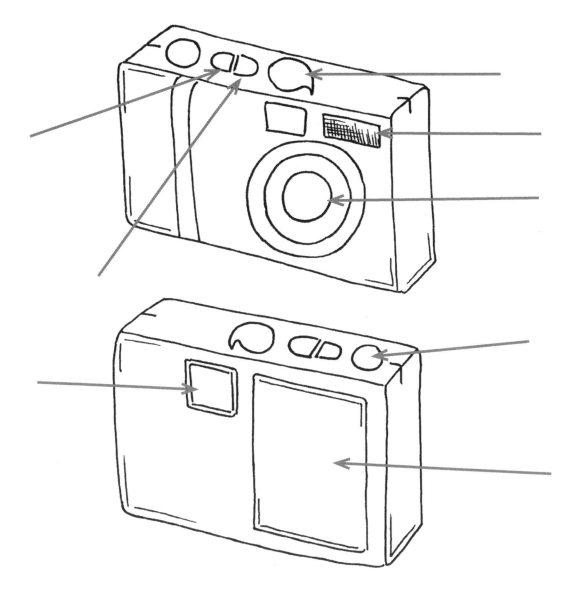

Name: _____

Write the speech in the speech bubbles.

Celebrations – teachers' notes

Learning Objective
To select and use different techniques to communicate ideas through pictures.

Curriculum Links
Religious Education

- Reflect on stories and their meanings
- Explore how beliefs and practices can be expressed through language and artistic forms
- Use technology to express their views.

ICT can support the teacher in helping children to feel empathy. It is important for children to learn to see the world though others' eyes and from other points of view. Careful teacher-led ICT activities can encourage children to reflect on issues and gain a deeper understanding about other people's beliefs.

Computers are useful tools for investigative work, both in the classroom and at home. They allow the children to interpret information from a variety of sources for themselves quickly and easily. A carefully designed RE, ICT task can provide opportunities for the children to exercise their imagination and express their feelings on issues in original ways.

Activity One – Rangoli Patterns

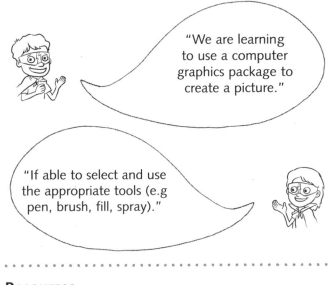

"We are learning to use a computer graphics package to create a picture."

"If able to select and use the appropriate tools (e.g pen, brush, fill, spray)."

Resources
- 'Rangoli Patterns' activity sheet
- Computers
- Scanner
- Printer
- Digital projector
- Interactive Whiteboard
- Laptop
- A1 paper.

Introduction

Read the celebrations story to the class. What are they celebrating? How are they celebrating? Explain that this celebration is known as Diwali which is one of the main festivals of India and the Hindu religion. Drawing rangoli designs is part of the Diwali celebrations. Rangoli means row of colours and rangoli designs are passed down through generations, with some of them being hundreds of years old.

Tell the children they are going to make rangoli pattern research posters. Split the class into small groups. Ask the children to search for and look at a variety of rangoli patterns. Encourage them to find the names of these patterns, such as the rising sun, the moon, stars and people dancing. Other popular themes are natural images such as, birds, creepers, elephants, fish, the lotus flower and trees.

Print out samples of the different patterns and stick them onto A1 paper. Explain that while geometric patterns are very popular the motif of the lotus flower is frequently used. Ask the children to find images of the lotus flower and its leaves and add this to their rangoli pattern research poster.

Main Activity

Load the rangoli patterns activity sheet into a drawing program such as Paint. Ask the children to draw the outline shapes of the lotus leaf and to fill in with various rangoli designs. Remind them they can use their research posters to help them. Explain to the children they can experiment using different colours. Demonstrate how to do this on your own design using the digital projector and Interactive Whiteboard.

Allow children to experiment whilst making their designs.

Plenary

Ask the children to write a few sentences on how they made their patterns and explain what tools they used.

Encourage them to describe the effects they produced.

Print out their designs and put them on display.

Extension

If time permits, let the children draw their rangoli designs on their hands, using washable water paint. Remember to get the necessary permissions from home to do this.

Activity Two – Light and Dark

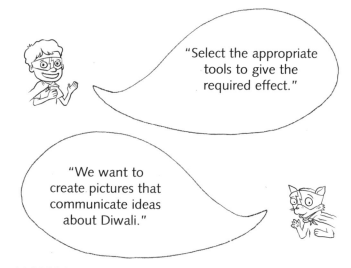

"Select the appropriate tools to give the required effect."

"We want to create pictures that communicate ideas about Diwali."

Resources

- 'Celebrations' story
- 'Light and Dark' activity sheet
- Scanner
- Computers
- Printer
- Digital projector
- Interactive Whiteboard
- Laptop
- Diva lamp.

Introduction

Dim the lights; light a diva lamp and read the 'Celebrations' story to the class. Tell them this is the Diwali story. Explain Diwali is sometimes called the 'Festival of Light'. It takes place around the end of October and the beginning of November. Explain Diwali is celebrated with sitar music, Diwali cards, new and colourful clothes and very often fireworks.

Brainstorm the word 'light' and then 'darkness'. What feelings are associated with each word? List their ideas.

Do they like being in a room when it is dark, or do they prefer it when the room is light? Do they like it outside when it is dark? Ask the children to try and describe darkness. Ask them to describe light.

Consider light as a symbol. Tell the children that darkness is often used as a symbol of evil and light is a symbol of good. Why do they think this is? Why do they think light is an important symbol in late autumn?

Ask what lights are associated with the festival of Diwali. Show the children the diva that was lit during the telling of the story. Tell them divas are lit during Diwali. They are usually made of clay, and ghee (which is clarified butter or oil) is used as fuel, cotton wool is sometimes used as a wick. What do they represent? Explain that sometimes light is a symbol of good defeating darkness.

Main Activity

Tell the children they are going to make Diwali pictures on the computer using the pictures of the diva on the 'Light and Dark' activity sheet. Upload the activity sheet into a drawing program, like Paint. Discuss the use of black and colour on the screen and in print.

Introduce the idea of painting with light. Demonstrate how to use the spray tool to select colours and patterns to colour the picture of the diva in. Ask the children to use the flood fill tool to create a black background and then to use the mark making tool and various colours to explore the quality of light and colour on the background and for the flame of the diva.

Plenary

Discuss the advantages and disadvantages of using ICT. If they did not use the computers how could they have used similar effects? Explain they could have used wax crayons and scraping techniques to produce similar effects. Encourage them to try out these traditional methods on the 'Light and Dark' activity sheet. Display the results of both methods and discuss the similarities and differences.

The children's finished digital Diwali pictures can be exchanged with children in other schools by email, to reinforce the idea that an image on screen can be the final product.

Extension

Ask the children to create their own pictures of Ravana, the demon king, using the draw and fill tools in a drawing program such as Paint. This could be done as homework.

Activity Three – Good and Evil

"To gain an understanding that work can be easily amended and ideas can be tried without spoiling an earlier version."

"If able to edit and save."

Resources

- 'Celebrations' story
- 'Good and Evil' activity sheet
- Scanner
- Computers
- Printer
- Digital projector
- Interactive whiteboard
- Laptop
- Word Art.

Good	Evil
Admirable	Aggressive
Bold	Arrogant
Brave	Bad
Calm	Bossy
Caring	Brutal
Dedicated	Cruel
Determined	Demanding
Friendly	Destructive
Generous	Dishonest
Gentle	Fierce
Giving	Horrible
Honest	Manipulative
Kind	Mean
Loving	Obnoxious
Loyal	Rude
Polite	Selfish
Reliable	Threatening
Trusting	Wicked
Virtuous	Wrong

Introduction

Read the 'Celebrations' story to the class. Ask the children to tell you who the evil characters are? Why is Ravana evil? Is Marchia evil? Who are the good characters? What do these characters do that show they are bad or good? How does good defeat evil in the Celebration story of Rama and Sita?

Ask the children to think of stories they have heard and any films or television programmes they have watched where good defeats evil. Encourage them to name the evil characters in these stories. In what ways are they evil? Name the good characters in these stories. In what ways are they good? What do they think would have happened if the bad characters had won in these stories?

What were they celebrating at the end of the 'Celebrations' story? Ask if they think it is a good idea to celebrate that good has defeated evil?

Main Activity

Provide a list of adjectives which describe character. You could use the list above or ideas of your own, taking into consideration the previous knowledge and ability of the class. These words can also be added to by using a Thesaurus.

Discuss the meaning of the words. Ask the children to pick out words which describe Rama and Sita such as, honest, brave, loyal, determined. Ask if they think it is difficult to be like Rama or Sita? Ask the children to pick out words which describe Ravana.

Use the 'Good and Evil' activity sheet and ask the children to write the words that match the character's personality around the appropriate character. Ask the children to choose one of the words and demonstrate how to type the word into WordArt and edit the text by changing the font and size. Then show them how to format the text and to change the different fill effects.

Ask the children to choose one of the good qualities and one of the evil qualities they identified on their 'Good and Evil' activity sheet. Using WordArt they should choose a style, change the font make it large enough to fill an A4 size piece of paper, change colours, use the preset fills and experiment with their own. Remind the children to save their work as they go along.

Plenary

Make large pictures of Rama and Sita and Ravana. Ask groups of children to paint them for display. Ask the class to print out their WordArt words and pin them up next to the appropriate character. Ask:

- Why does this quality suit this character?
- Can they indicate where about in the story it showed this?

Extension

Ask the children to consider what good things can be said about them. What characters from the celebration story are they like?

Use the 'Enlightenment' activity sheet. Split the class into small groups. Ask them to print and stick on a photo of someone in their group. If a photo is not all ready available use a digital camera to take one. Ask them to write down three good things about this person and three things which are not so good about the person's character. Explain they need to be sensitive to the other people's feelings when they do this.

How did it feel to have good things said about you?

How does it feel to have bad things said about you? Could they be more like Rama and Sita? Can they change the bad things about them? How?

Activity Four – Diwali

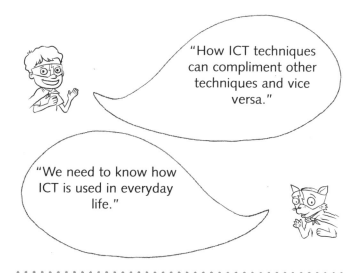

"How ICT techniques can compliment other techniques and vice versa."

"We need to know how ICT is used in everyday life."

Resources

- 'Celebrations' story
- 'Enlightenment' activity sheet
- 'Diwali' activity sheet
- Computers
- Printer
- Digital projector
- Interactive Whiteboard
- Laptop
- Card
- Silver paper.

Introduction

Read the 'Celebrations' story to the class. Explain that during Diwali people send Diwali cards and gifts to each other. Explain traditionally these cards are made from Banyan leaves that have pictures painted on them.

Tell the children that nowadays Diwali e-cards are becoming increasingly popular, as it is fast, instantaneous and cost effective. The use of Java and Flash technology has helped to make e-cards more vibrant and interactive, such as cards that feature virtual bursting crackers, exploding fireworks and flickering diva flames. Show the children examples by searching the Internet for online sites.

Main Activity

Tell the children they are going to produce their own Diwali cards. This can be done as an e-card or by finding suitable animated gifs, ClipArt images and rangoli designs, printing them out and sticking them onto card.

They could also use WordArt to write 'Happy Diwali' to stick inside their cards. If you wish you could add other decorations such as ribbons, sequins and glitter to enhance their cards.

Plenary

Discuss why they have added the different ClipArt and decorations to their cards.

Extension

Use the Diwali activity sheet to decorate and make a Diwali gift box. If you make Diwali sweets in the classroom they can be put inside the box to take home.

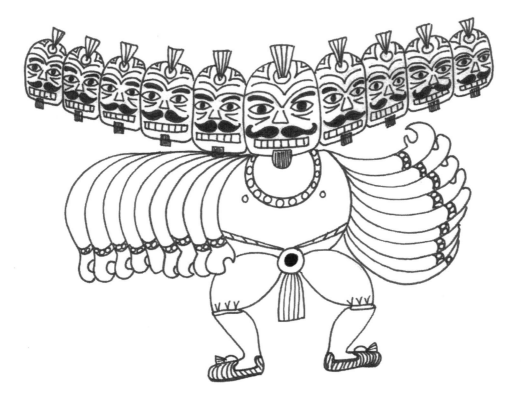

There was a time, long, long ago, when the land was ruled by evil demons. The most evil demon of them all was Ravana, the demon King. He had twenty arms and ten heads. Ravana lived in a magnificent palace across the ocean on the Island of Lanka.

One day Ravana was walking in his amazing gardens talking to his advisor, Marchia. "I've heard there is a beautiful woman living in the forest on the mainland," Ravana said.

"If you are talking about Sita she is indeed very beautiful," said Marchia.

"I would like to see this woman with my own eyes," Ravana said, rubbing his hands together.

So Marchia showed Ravana the way to Rama and Sita's cottage on the mainland. They hid in the trees and watched as Rama and Sita sat outside the cottage chatting to Rama's brother, Laksham.

"She is more beautiful than I thought," Ravana said. "I think I will marry her."

"But, she won't ever leave Rama," said Marchia.

"I don't care," said Ravana and shook his twenty fists in the air. "I will kidnap her and make her my wife."

Marchia looked very worried. "You already have over two hundred wives," he said, trying to keep his voice steady. "I beg you, as your oldest friend and advisor, don't make Rama angry by stealing his wife."

Ravana roared with all ten mouths in his ten heads. "I am the demon king and will take what I want. You have two choices, lure Rama away, or die a gruesome death," Ravana growled. All his eyes glowed orange with rage.

Marchia quaked in his boots and bowed his head. "Rama will kill us all," he mumbled to himself.

Even so, he changed himself immediately into a beautiful golden deer, because he would rather die by Rama's hand than be tortured to death by Ravana. The demon king hid himself behind the trees and watched Marchia gallop toward the cottage.

Outside the cottage, Rama and Sita were still chatting to Laksham, when Sita spotted Marchia disguised as the magnificent golden deer.

"Oh look Rama!" Sita pointed at the deer. "That's the most enchanting deer I've ever seen. Will you catch it for me? I'd love to have it as a pet."

Rama smiled. "I'll do anything for you, my love."

Rama stood up and Laksham put his hand on his shoulder.

"That's not a good idea brother. There are many evil things lurking in the forest it might be a trick," Laksham said.

"It will be all right brother, you stay here and look after my wife while I go and catch the deer. I'm sure everything will be fine," Rama said.

The deer darted into the forest and Rama chased after it as fast as he could. Sita and Laksham waited for his return. Soon Sita began pacing up and down outside the cottage.

"He's taking a long time. Maybe you should go look for him," she said to Laksham.
"I promised my brother I would look after you," he replied.

"I am worried something has happened to him. I would feel a lot happier if you went to check," Sita said.

"If you insist," Laksham said. "But, before I go, I am going to draw a magic circle around the cottage. As long as you stay inside the circle, you'll be safe."

He drew a large magical circle around the cottage and set off into the forest to look for Rama. As soon as Laksham was out of sight, Ravana emerged from his hiding place dressed in a hooded, long robe. He was pleased his plan was working and Sita was now sat alone outside the cottage. He bent double and hobbled toward her carrying an empty bowl.

When Sita saw him she jumped up and ran to the edge of the magic circle.

"I'm a simple holy man. I've had nothing to eat for days. Have you got a little bit of food to spare," Ravana said.

"Oh you poor man, come to the house I will give you some food," she said.

"I am so tired from walking all day. I will rest on this rock and you can bring it to me." Ravana sat on a large rock.

Sita ran into the cottage and found some food for the old man to eat. Without even thinking she rushed back to the holy man. As soon as she had crossed the magic circle Ravana threw back his robes, revealing his ten heads. He grabbed Sita.

"You're coming with me across the ocean to my palace on the Island of Lanka and you will be my queen," he roared.

"No! No!" Sita screeched.

She struggled to get away but, Ravana had too tight a grip with his ten pairs of hands.

"Rama, save me! Help!" Sita cried.

But, it was no good Rama could not hear her. By the time he had returned to the cottage she was all ready far, far away. Rama and Laksham searched everywhere for her. For weeks and weeks Rama continued his search, long after everyone else had given up. One day he met Hanuman the monkey king.

Illustration of Hanuman the monkey king.

"I am looking for my wife she disappeared from our cottage months ago," Rama said. He described his wife to Hanuman.

"I saw a woman matching that description being dragged past here by Ravana. He was taking her to his palace." Hanuman said. "I will check if it is your wife and take a message to her for you."

"Thank you. Give my ring to Sita if you find her. If it is really her she will recognise it" Rama handed Hanuman his ring.

At the palace, Hanuman slipped past the guards and hid amongst the lotus flowers in the palace gardens. He could see Sita sitting very proud and Ravana's heads moving fiercely as he yelled and shouted at her.

"I've waited long enough. Be sensible and become my queen. Rama will never rescue you. You might as well forget him," Ravana growled.

"Rama will come and then you will be sorry," Sita said.

"If you don't marry me I will kill you and let's see Rama save a dead body. You have three more days to decide." He thumped a flower pot and it shattered into tiny pieces.

Ravana stormed off and Sita burst into tears. Hanuman crept out of his hiding place amongst the lotus flowers.

"Don't cry," he said. "I've bought this ring as a message from your husband. As soon as he knows where you've been hidden, he will defeat Ravana."

Sita stopped crying and smiled. She knew her husband would come for her. "Take my necklace to prove that you've found me!" She handed her necklace to Hanuman.

Hanuman raced back to Rama and gave him the necklace. Rama was so pleased his wife had been found at last. Hanuman guided Rama to Ravana's palace. When they arrived Rama was shocked and angry to see how ill his beautiful wife looked. He saw Ravana yelling and shaking his fists at her. Without hesitation, Rama leapt in front of Ravana, sword drawn.

"What have you done to my wife? Prepare to die," he said.

Before Ravana could speak Rama plunged his sword through his heart. Ravana dropped to the ground.

"You've killed him," Sita flung her arms around her husband. "Thank you. You have saved me."

"I'll take you home. Don't worry he can never hurt you again," Rama said and kissed his wife.

The whole world rejoiced that good had triumphed over evil. The reign of the demons was finally over. Every home lit an oil lamp in their window to welcome Rama and Sita home and celebrate their happiness.

The End

Rangoli Patterns

Name: _____

- Draw your own rangoli patterns on the hand.
- Use your research to help you.

- What tools did you use to produce these effects?

_____

_____

_____

_____

Name: _____

Use the computer to make your own light and dark Diwali pictures.

Name: _____

Write what the characters are like in the space around them.
Are they good or evil?

Name: _____

- Add a photograph in the frame.
- Write some good and bad qualities in the boxes.

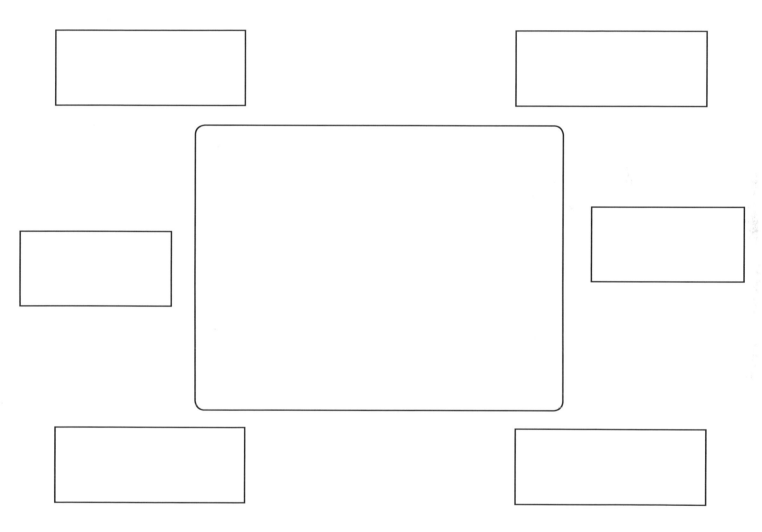

- How did it feel to have good things said about you?

_____

_____

- How does it feel to have bad things said about you?

_____

_____

Diwali

Name: _____

- Decorate and make the Diwali box.
- Fill it with Diwali sweets and gifts to celebrate Diwali.

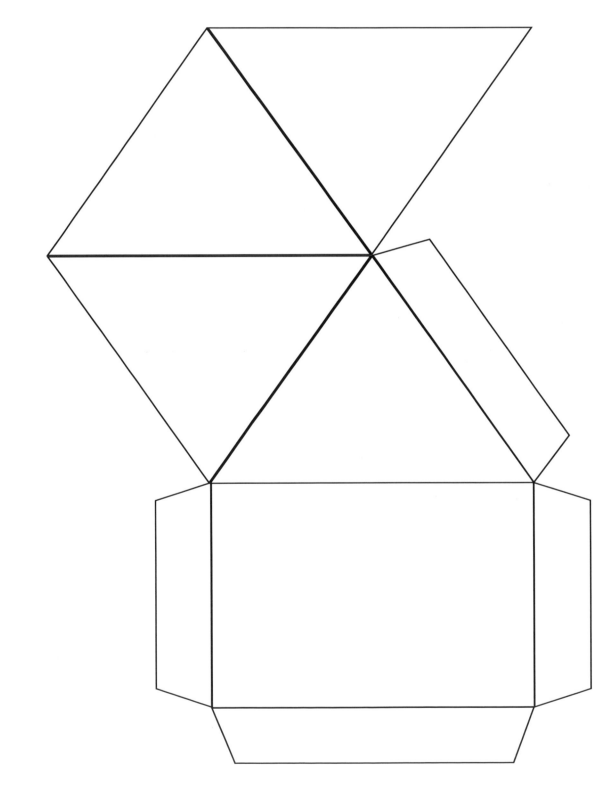

Why do we Remember? – teachers' notes

Learning Objective

To use appropriate search techniques to find information.

Curriculum Links

History

- Find out about significant events from the past
- Use straightforward lines of enquiry
- Use the Internet and other digital sources to find out about significant events and people.

The use of search engines on the Internet can compliment the use of books as a way of gaining access to museum collections, buildings and artefacts. CD-ROMS can also provide a useful resource but, it is understandable that it can prove expensive to get licenses to allow a whole class access at the same time and so are not as convenient as the Internet.

Children can apply what they learn about using these electronic sources to all areas of the curriculum. But, it is important to be aware that there are other methods of collecting data such as visiting a museum or place of historical interest and interviewing people about their experiences and expertise. For this reason this chapter gives children the experience of researching information in a wide variety of ways.

Activity One – Going on a Visit

"We are learning to use the digital camera and upload the pictures to the computer."

Resources

- 'Why do we Remember?' story
- 'Going on a Visit' activity sheet
- Computers
- Printer
- Digital projector
- Whiteboard
- Laptop
- Digital camera

- YouTube extract of Remembrance Day ceremony in London: http://www.youtube.com/watch?v=yeLICzVb0hk
- Books on WWI.

Introduction

Read the story, 'Why do we Remember?' to the class. Explain the story took place during WWI. Tell them they have war memorials to honour and commemorate all the soldiers that died during the war. Show them pictures of the Cenotaph on the Internet where the Queen lays a wreath on Remembrance Day.

Watch a news video or YouTube extract of the ceremony. Point out the main features, such as laying of the wreaths, the two minute silence, the march, the music, the involvement of the Royal family and Government officials. Tell the children the soldiers are wearing their uniforms and medals and have poppies on, like the soldiers in the 'Why do we Remember?' story.

Ask the children have they ever been to a Remembrance Day ceremony like Adam. Why did they go? Point out Adam went because he was a Cub Scout and was part of the parade. How did the ceremony they attended compare to the one Adam went to and the one they saw in the video clips you showed them?

Arrange a visit to the local war memorial. It is a good idea to check beforehand if anyone in the class has people they know or ancestors they may be able to trace. This can provide a good discussion point for the class but, will need to be handled sensitively. Ensure you have the necessary permissions before going on the trip.

Tell the children they are going to be finding out information about their own local war memorial. Encourage the children to describe what they see and take digital photographs. Tally the names. Ask the children to make notes of any surnames that appear more than once. Discuss how people with the same surname might be related to each other. Identify families who lost more than one person.

Ask the children probing questions to get them to think and look for the evidence available on their visit. Use the questions on the 'Going on a Visit' activity sheet as starters. What information can they find? What information is not available? How can they find out the answers to the questions on the 'Going on a Visit' activity sheet?

Main Activity

Back in the classroom encourage the children to upload the photographs to the computer by plugging the digital cameras in to a USB port. Ensure they save each picture with a different file name so they can easily be identified. Some children may require assistance to achieve this.

Explain they are going to create a PowerPoint presentation using the images. The children can sequence their photos and give their opinions on what they saw. Encourage the children to write a sentence on each slide to explain the photograph they took. Demonstrate how to crop their photos to make the pictures more central. It may be necessary to limit the amount of slides to about six to eight.

Plenary

Provide time for the children to show their PowerPoint presentations and ask each other appropriate questions about the information they found out and about how they made their presentation, such as

- What went well?
- How could they make them better?

Extension

Provide the children with a selection of books. Ask the children to find out why poppies are used to commemorate the soldiers who died in World War One by using the books. Point out the index and contents pages to help them with their search for information.

Activity Two – Using the Internet

"We are learning how to use a search engine for straightforward lines of enquiry."

"Good use of menus, indexes and keywords to gather information."

"Search engines are an important source of information."

Resources

- 'Why do we Remember?' story
- 'Using the Internet' activity sheet
- Computers
- Search engine
- Printer
- Digital projector
- Whiteboard
- Laptop.

Selection of websites with images of war memorials and information on where they are located

Selection of websites with a variety of menus such as:

- www.britishmuseum.org menu is at bottom of screen
- www.britishlegion.org.uk menu is across the top and displays more options on left-hand side
- www.nhm.ac.uk menu expands if rests curser on it
- www.london.iwm.org.uk menu on left-hand side and gives more options if you click on an item.

A selection of websites to use with the Using the Internet activity sheet, such as: the CBBC News website, Woodlands Junior School in Kent and the Imperial War Museum. Please check these sites to determine their suitability with your class before use.

Introduction

Read the 'Why do we Remember?' story to the class. Remind them the local war memorial helps us remember the people who died in wars all over the world. Ask if other countries, cities, towns and villages have war memorials. How can they find out? Tell them about other events in the World such as, Anzac day in New Zealand and Australia on the 25th April to commemorate the Gallipoli landing in 1916.

Recap how information can be found on visits, in books and on CD-ROMs. What other ways can we find out about the past? Explain the function of Internet search engines is to find information quickly and easily on the World Wide Web.

Search for images of other war memorials and monuments. Project large images of them onto a whiteboard and point out where they are situated and what wars they commemorate. Point out that you used the key words 'war memorial' to help you search for what you wanted. It is a good idea to check the websites first before the lesson begins to make sure the material is appropriate for your class and ensure the lesson runs smoothly.

Explain it is possible to follow the highlighted hyperlinks to find out more information. Show the children how to use the back key to return to the previous page.

Main Activity

Explain to the class that when using the Internet information can be found by looking at the menu. Show examples of menus from different websites, such as your own school website. Demonstrate when the curser is rested on some menus, they open out to display more options. Ensure you have checked this before the lesson begins to make sure the lesson runs smoothly.

Split the class into small groups. Ask them to search for information about WWI, using key words such as: Remembrance Day, war memorials, the cenotaph, armistice, poppies, etc. Identify three websites on the Using the Internet activity sheet and ask the children to mark on a scale of 1-5, with 5 being the best. Encourage the children to consider what they thought of the websites layout, how easy it was to

find their way around and how easy it was to read and understand.

Plenary

Come back together as a while class and ask each group to report back their opinions of the sites explored. Which site was the best? Which did they like least? Did they find any other sites they liked?

Ask the children to explain the function of hyperlinks. Discuss the advantages and disadvantages of using search engines and websites to find information.

Extension

The children could make posters advertising the use of the best website they found, which gave them information about WWI. This could be the sites they looked at using the keywords.

Activity Three – Interviews

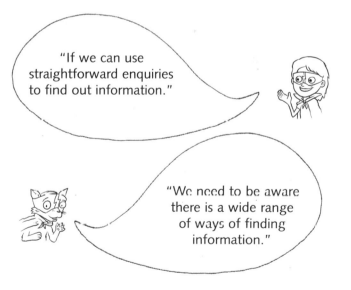

"If we can use straightforward enquiries to find out information."

"We need to be aware there is a wide range of ways of finding information."

Resources

- 'Why do we Remember?' story
- 'Interviews' activity sheet
- Computers
- Printer
- Digital projector
- Whiteboard
- Laptop

- Digital recorders
- Digital camera
- Visitors, such as: veterans, grandparents who may have been a child during the WWII, evacuees, soldiers, family of soldiers, etc.

Introduction

Read the story, 'Why do we Remember' to the class. Explain the story took place during WWI, but since then there have been many other wars which have taken lots of lives. Ask someone to come and talk to the children about their experiences in a war.

Before the visit, ask the children to work with a partner to think of three questions they would like to ask the person, or people, visiting. They should type these questions up on the computer and print them out leaving space to write the answers given. The children will need to know a little about the speakers beforehand so they are able to make the questions relevant.

Main Activity

Depending on the size of the school and how many people you can get to come into school you could try several different ideas for interviewing people about their experiences of war:

1. A single person could come in with any photos or artefacts and talk to the whole class. Encourage the children to make notes during the talk and ask questions at the end.
2. A panel of experts who briefly introduce themselves and then the children ask their prepared questions. Encourage the children to make notes on the panels answers.
3. Six or more experts around the hall, or room, and the children in groups of two or three go from person to person asking their questions and making notes of the answers given. The children may need clipboards.

If possible, record the people talking using digital recorders, so it can be listened back to by the whole class at a later date. Take the visitors' photographs to be used in any follow-up work.

Plenary

The children should share what they found out with the whole class. Discuss how they could find more information about what they found out and the types of resources available to find this information.

Extension

Some children can to write up their findings using a word processor and add a photo of the visitor and pictures of any artefacts they bought in.

Activity Four – Comparisons

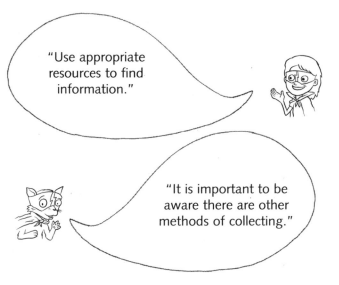

"Use appropriate resources to find information."

"It is important to be aware there are other methods of collecting."

Resources
- 'Why do we Remember?' story
- 'Comparisons' activity sheet
- Computers
- Printer
- Digital projector
- Whiteboard
- Laptop.

Introduction

Read the 'Why do we Remember?' story to the class. Point out Adam was wearing a poppy. Who else in the story was wearing a poppy? Ask the children why they think people wear poppies. Tell them poppies are worn on and around the 11th November. This is known as Remembrance Day.

Ask the children what sort of things do we remember on Remembrance Day? Ask the children who did Adam remember. Why? Explain, we remember the people who fought in the wars as a sign of respect for them.

Main Activity

Split the class into small groups. Set the children a research challenge linked to the 'Why do we Remember?' story, such as:

- When is Remembrance Day?
- Why do people wear poppies?
- What is Armistice Day?
- Why do we have a two minute silence?

Allow time for the children to use different sources to research these questions.

Ask the children to spend some time brainstorming what sort of information they were able to gather from the different sources:

- A visit
- Books
- Internet
- Talking to experts.

Which method did they prefer? Use the 'Comparisons' activity sheet to record their ideas and preferences.

Plenary

Discuss the advantages and disadvantages of using different types of sources for information. Explain to the children it is good to use different methods to research things.

Extension

Ask the children to list the places they found their information.

Why do we Remember?

Adam stood at the war memorial.

"You have to stand in silence for two minutes and think about the people who died in the First World War," Moose, the Cub Scout leader, warned his patrol.

Adam groaned. What was he going to think about? He didn't know anybody who died in the War.

"In complete silence," Moose repeated.

Adam bit his lip and stopped himself from telling Moose he was way too young to remember anyone who had died in the war, especially World War One. After all, he was only eight years old. But, he had to think about something – two minutes was a long, long time. He played with the poppy pinned to his Cub Scout uniform, twiddling it round and round. He noticed Moose's poppy was hanging upside down.

Adam thought. He remembered his Dad had told him stories about his Great-Grandad John who had fought in World War One. But, he hadn't died. He had come back home and lived till he was in his eighties. Adam tried to think of some of the stories his Dad had told him.

* * *

It was December 24th 1914. Great-Grandad John sat huddled in a muddy trench with his best-friend Reggie. They were only just seventeen years old. John's stomach rumbled but there was no time to eat. Soon it would be their turn to go over the trench wall to fight the Germans. The shells continued to thunder, illuminating the sky.

"Nearly midnight," Reggie said and shivered. John leant against the sandbags and nodded. His teeth chattered. Then to John's surprise the guns went silent. He wiggled his finger in his ears to see if he'd gone deaf. No. The shelling had definitely stopped. The silence was eerie. It made John feel colder than he all ready was.

"What's that noise?" Reggie whispered.

John strained to hear. Being carried on the breeze from the German trenches was singing. It was quiet at first but, it got louder and louder. John's skin tingled. The Germans were singing Christmas carols. One song after another echoed over 'No Man's Land'. John heard one he recognised. Reggie recognised it too and started to join in.

"Silent night, holy night," sang Reggie. The rest of the British troops started to join in. Soon, the German and British soldiers were singing in perfect harmony. It was beautiful.

The sky started to get lighter. John used his home-made periscope to peer over the top of the trench. He gasped and nudged Reggie. Some of the German and British soldiers were wandering about in 'No Man's Land', shaking hands, comparing uniforms and some were even huddled together in small groups having their photos taken.

"Come on, let's go meet them," John said to Reggie.

Reggie leapt to his feet and they both scrambled over the top. A German soldier walked up to them and offered them a piece of chocolate. John smiled. It had been months since he tasted chocolate. They tried to communicate with the

Germans with hand gestures and actions. It was difficult because neither of them spoke German.

Suddenly there was a loud cheer. One of the German soldiers ran into the clearing holding a football. John quickly put his helmet down on the frozen ground as a goal post. Reggie put his down as the other post. At the other end two German helmets were placed as the German goal. It was hard to believe these men had been trying to kill each other just a few hours before. Reggie scored the first goal. The Germans scored the next two.

* * *

Adam's Dad had told him that the soldiers all got into a lot of trouble over that football game. The officers were not happy they were being friendly with the enemy. They were ordered never to do it again.

The Mayor stood by the war memorial. "We should remember the people who gave their lives fighting for their country," he said.

This reminded Adam of another story his Dad had told him about his Great-Grandad John. It happened a few years after the football game.

* * *

Reggie had been sent over the wall to fight and hadn't returned. John knew he must be out there in 'No Man's Land' injured. He had to go find him. It was dark and the stretcher bearers had all ready been and come back. But, they had not seen any sign of Reggie.

John walked up to his senior officer and asked, "Please Sir, Reggie isn't back yet. Can I go look for him?"

The officer looked him up and down. "If he's not back soldier he's probably dead."

"I don't' believe he's dead, Sir," John could feel the tears welling up in his eyes. "I have to go find him. He is probably injured and waiting for me to help him."

"But, you'll be putting your own life at risk."

"I'm sure he would do the same for me," John said.

The officer looked at him in silence. After what felt like ages to John he said, "Go, if you must."

"Thank you, Sir. Thank you." John grinned and rushed over the trench wall to find Reggie.

John searched all over 'No Man's Land' in the dark and eventually found his friend.

"Reggie." John shook him. "It's me."

Reggie opened his eyes and shut them again. He was badly wounded and blood poured from his chest. He was drifting in and out of consciousness.

"Reggie, wake up," John whispered.

"John, I knew you would come," Reggie said and reached out to him.

"Yes I'm here. I've got you now," John said. John wiped the tears from his cheeks and lifted his best friend over his shoulder. He carried Reggie back to the trench where he could get medical attention.

All the way, his friend kept saying over and over, "I knew you would come for me. I knew it."

But, Reggie's wound was too severe. There was nothing the medics could do for him. John cradled his friend's head and cried, as he slowly slipped away and died.

* * *

"We should wear our poppies with pride," said the Mayor.

Adam looked at his poppy. The green paper leaf had fallen off where he had been playing with it. There were lots of soldiers in their uniforms wearing medals. They had poppies on too. These soldiers had fought in different wars to his Great-Grandad John. He wondered if their friends had died in battle too like Reggie did in the First World War. Was that why they wore their poppies with pride?

Adam stared up at the war memorial covered with lists of names of people who had died during all the different wars. People lay wreaths of poppies and wooden crosses around the memorial stone.

Lest we forget

The clock struck eleven. It was time for the two minutes silence. Moose put his hands together and bowed his head. Adam put his hands together and bowed his head too. He was going to think about all the people who died in war, even though he never knew them.

The End

Name: _____

- Add a photo of your local war monument.

┌───┐
│   │
│   │
│   │
│   │
│   │
│   │
│   │
│   │
│   │
│   │
└───┘

- Which war did the soldiers listed on the monument die in?

_____

_____

- Who built the war memorial?

_____

_____

- What do the symbols on the monument mean?

_____

_____

_____

Using the Internet

Name: _____

- What do you think of the websites you have looked at?
- Fill in the table below:

Website	Layout	How easy is it to find your way around	How easy is it to read and understand
	1-5	1-5	1-5

- Which website did you like best?

_____

- Why?

_____

- Which website did you like least?

_____

- Why?

_____

- Did you find any other sites you liked? Why did you like them?

_____

_____

Name: _____

- Who is visiting today _____

- Think of three questions you would like to ask the visitor.

- Write your questions below:

Question	Write their answer here:
1.	
2.	
3.	

- What did you find out?

_____

_____

_____

_____

Comparisons

Name: _____

- Write what information you found out from the different sources.

Visit	
Books	
Internet	
Experts	
Other	

- What method did you like best?

_____

- Why?

_____

_____

Learning Objective

To create, test, modify and store instructions to control the movement of floor and screen turtles.

Curriculum Links

Geography

- Gain an understanding of the uses and functions of maps
- Make links with their own locality and other places
- Consider issues affecting communities.

Activity One – In Order

"We are learning to program Roamer."

Resources

- 'Robot Postman' story
- 'Right and Left' activity sheet
- Digital projector
- Whiteboard
- Laptop

Introduction

Read the 'Robot Postman' story to the class. Ask the children what they think the postmen did wrong. Why was the robot unable to deliver the letters? Ask the children, what did Ciara and Sean tell them to do. How did this help?

Ask the children to show you which is their right hand and which is their left hand. Why do they think the postmen got it wrong? Split the class into pairs and demonstrate how when they are facing each other, their left is the opposite of their partners.

Point out when programming Roamer they should be facing the same direction as they want Roamer to go. Ask the children to suggest ways they can remember which is their left and which, is their right, such as: 'I write with my right hand.'

Use the 'Right and Left' activity sheet to record their ideas.

Main Activity

Discuss the basic floor instructions followed by the turtle and demonstrate how to input these instructions. Tell them how to clear the memory by pressing the CM button twice. Explain they should enter the instructions one at a time in the correct order.

Place objects in front of, behind and to the left and right of Roamer. The objects should be positioned so the children are only required to give two or three instructions to move the turtle to the correct position. Ensure the objects are placed in positions that do not require difficult angles.

Explain that the floor turtle can only move in the direction and how far they tell it to. Discuss how two separate instructions can produce the same results, such as: forward 1 and forward 3 is the same as forward 4.

Ask the children to predict the instructions they will need to input to make the floor turtle move. Then test their predictions.

Plenary

Explain it is important to follow instructions in the correct order. Tell them it is also important that they start in the correct place else the instructions do not work. Ask what they think would happen if the Robot Postman started at the school instead of the Post Office. Explain the instructions would have to be different.

Extension

Challenge the children to move the Roamer in a square or staircase movement.

Activity Two – Map

"If the instructions are given in the right order."

"We need to understand how many electrical devices work by following instructions in the correct order."

Resources

• 'Robot Postman' story
• 'Map' activity sheet
• Computers
• Printer
• Digital projector
• Whiteboard
• Laptop

Introduction

Read the 'Robot Postman' story to the class. Tell them they are going to pretend to be robot postman. Remind them they must give their instructions in order. Ask them what might happen if they do not put the instructions in the correct order. Remind them what happened to postman Paul and Postman Pete when they did not put the instructions into the robot correctly.

Main Activity

Using the ideas from the classroom ask the children to work in small groups of 4-5 children and mark out their own map designs on the playground using chalk. If the weather is not suitable to do this outside it may be possible to use the hall and mark out the route with skipping ropes, string or masking tape, etc. If using tape ensure you clear it with the caretaker, especially if he has only just polished the floor.

Tell the children to check they have included in their map all the places mentioned in the story. Ask them to choose one member of the group to be the Robot Postman. The children should work together in their group to give instructions to move the person they choose as the Robot Postman around the map. Explain they have to standardise their steps so one step is the same each time. How can they do this? Tell them to start each time from the Post Office.

Ask the children to record their ideas using the grid on the 'Map' activity sheet.

Plenary

Allow time for the children to compare their maps and observe each group give the instructions to deliver the post.

Ask the children what other electronic things work by following instructions. Discuss the use of remote controls or the control dials on a dishwasher or washing machine cycle. Explain to the children that even the kettle and the toaster are controlled electrical devices that work by following instructions in the correct order.

Extension

Encourage the children to write down their instructions and then move each group from map to map and see if they can follow the other groups' instructions.

Activity Three – Instructions

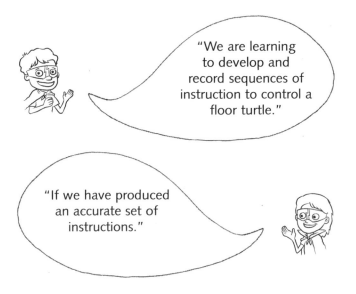

"We are learning to develop and record sequences of instruction to control a floor turtle."

"If we have produced an accurate set of instructions."

Resources

- 'Robot Postman' story
- 'Instructions' activity sheet
- Computers
- Printer
- Digital projector
- Whiteboard
- Laptop
- Floor Turtle.

Introduction

Read the 'Robot Postman' story to the class. Remind them instructions need to be carried out in the right order.

Help the children to draw a large floor map to map out the postman's route. Mark on the map some of the places mentioned in the story.

Explain to the children they are going to program a floor turtle to deliver the post to the places mentioned in the story. The turtle is going to be the Robot Postman. Tell the children they will need to use the arrow commands on the Roamer. Demonstrate how to move Roamer forward and backwards. Explain how to make Roamer move in a 90° right-angle turn, both left and right.

Main Activity

Encourage the children to write down their sequence of instructions to guide the turtle around the route. Point out the turtle will need to move along the route in straight lines or right-angled turns. Discuss how many degrees in a full circle and how many degrees in half and a quarter of a circle.

Explain they can write the instructions using abbreviations, such as: F=Forward, R=Right turn, etc. So they could list: F2, R90°, F2, etc.

Discuss with the children what a prediction is. Explain it is a good guess like an estimate. Tell the children they need to predict how many moves forwards the Roamer needs to take to get close to the place where they have to deliver the letters.

Ask the children to test their predictions to help them write their instructions. It is important to put a mark on the map where the Roamer is to start from, so they can start from the same place each time.

Plenary

Provide time for the children to demonstrate their instructions and discuss how they could improve them. Was the post delivered? If not how did the instructions need to be changed so the post was delivered correctly?

Extension

How was writing instructions for the Roamer different to giving instructions to each other? Was it harder or easier? What problems did they have?

Activity Four – Robots Today

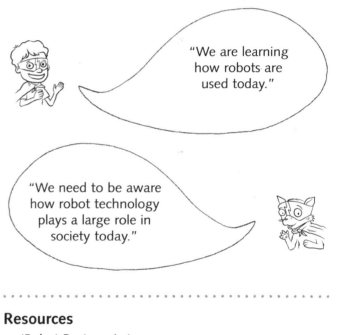

"We are learning how robots are used today."

"We need to be aware how robot technology plays a large role in society today."

Resources

- 'Robot Postman' story
- 'Robots Today' activity sheet
- Computers
- Printer
- Digital projector
- Whiteboard
- Laptop
- Search Engine.

Introduction

Read the 'Robot Postman' story to the class. Discuss with the class how robot technology is used throughout the world today.

Explain robots are used in production lines such as for building cars. Tell the children the Space Rover is a robot and it is visiting planets like Mars and sending back the data to Earth. It is safer for the robot to go and explore in this way than for humans to go. Military and police organizations use robots to assist in dangerous activities such as those used by bomb squads. Hospitals use robotic technology to help with surgical procedures. Ask the children to suggest their own ideas on how robots are and could be used.

Main Activity

Split the class into pairs. Ask them to research different ways robots are used in society today. Tell them they can use an Internet Search Engine to find information.

Encourage each pair to choose one way robots are used today and print images of the robot to stick on the 'Robots Today' activity sheet. They should also write and print out sentences on how this robot is used.

Plenary

Tell the children robots are designed to meet a need. Display the children's robotic activity sheets and discuss the wide variety of needs these devices have met.

Extension

Ask the children to identify a need and design their own robot to meet this need. Encourage the children to explain how they think their robot could be used in society today.

The phone rang.

"Hello," said Postman Pete.

There was an enormous sneeze on the other end of the phone. Postman Pete had to hold the receiver away from his ear it was so loud.

"Who's this?" Postman Pete said.

"It's me, Postman Penny," said a snuffly voice. "I can't come to work today because I'm ill." Postman Penny blew her nose. Postman Pete sighed. "You're the second person to ring in sick today."

He put the phone down and stared at the piles and piles of letters waiting to be sorted and delivered.

"I'm never going to be able to do all this on my own," he groaned.

"What's up?" a voice behind him asked.

Postman Pete jumped. Standing behind him was Postman Paul.

"It looks like we're the only two in today," Postman Pete said. "Postman Pat and Postman Penny have both phoned in sick."

"No problem," Postman Paul said.

"What do you mean, *No problem*? Look at all these letters and parcels." Postman Pete waved his hands at the packages. "We'll never get all these sorted and delivered before Christmas."

"Ahhh! That's because you haven't seen my surprise," Postman Paul said.

"Surprise?"

"Yes. Wait here." Postman Paul rushed out to his van and when he returned Postman Pete was amazed to see walking next to him was a man made of metal. On his chest was what looked like a control panel.

"Who? What?" Postman Pete stuttered.

"This is the Robot Postman," Postman Paul announced happily. "All we need to do is input our instructions and the Robot Postman will make all the deliveries for us in half the time."

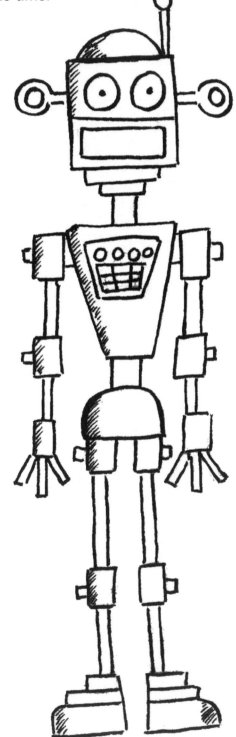

Postman Pete and Postman Paul got to work sorting all the mail.

When all the parcels were sorted, they started to program the robot. Postman Paul loaded all the letters into the Robot Postman's sack. Postman Pete input the commands on the control panel. When they were ready Postman Pete pressed *Go*. The Robot whirred into action and walked straight out of the Post office door. But, they did not watch to see which way the Robot Postman went.

Later that day Ciara and Sean were on their way home from school. They walked past the lake and were very surprised to see a whole load of envelopes floating on the surface of the water. Sean fished one out. It was addressed to Mr Gallagher, 54 The High Street.

"But, that is the other end of town," Ciara said.

"What's it doing in the lake?" Sean asked.

Ciara shrugged her shoulders. "Maybe we should take them back to the Post Office," she said.

Sean agreed. They both got all the soggy letters out of the lake and made their way toward the Post Office. They stopped when they saw old Mrs Carlin standing in the doorway of her house holding a package. She was looking up and down the street.

"What's the matter Mrs Carlin?" Sean asked.

"I found a parcel left on my doorstep," Mrs Carlin said. "But, it is not addressed to me. It is for Betty Finnegan who lives right the other side of town."

"That's strange," Ciara told her. "We found some letters for Mr Gallagher at 54, The High Street in the lake. We are taking them to the Post Office.

"We can take the parcel with us too," Sean said.

Mrs Carlin smiled and gave them the parcel. Ciara and Sean continued on their way to the Post Office.

"What's that?" Sean said pointing to the dustbin outside the park.

Ciara looked. She could see another parcel poking out the top of the dustbin. It had a big red ribbon tied around it.

"That doesn't look like rubbish at all," Ciara said.

Sean picked it up. "This parcel has been delivered to the wrong place too."

"We best take it back to the Post Office as well," Ciara said.

There was a group of people standing at the corner street. They waved envelopes and clutched packages. They all looked very angry.

"What's going on?" Sean asked.

"We were delivered the wrong post," said Mrs McCamphil, who worked at the supermarket. "I was expecting a very important letter from my daughter. I want to know where my post has gone."

"So do I," said Reverend Mahoney.

"We found these letters for Mr Gallagher in the lake," Ciara said. "We are taking them back to the Post Office."

"That's a good idea," Reverend Mahoney said.

The angry mob followed them to the Post Office.

At the Post Office Ciara, Sean and the angry mob were surprised to see a queue of people that went right out of the Post Office door.

They were all holding letters and parcels.

"What's going on?" Sean asked.

"We've all been delivered the wrong post," Jenny Pickles said.

Ciara looked at the other side of the road. Walking towards them was the Robot Postman, but instead of crossing the road and walking toward the Post Office it turned left and walked straight into a brick wall.

Sean laughed. "I think I know what happened," he said.

Sean crossed the road and led the Robot Postman into the post office. Postman Pete and Postman Paul were busy taking all the letters and parcels back from the people in the queue. They looked cross. When they saw the postman they started shouting at it for taking all the letters and parcels to the wrong places.

"It's not the robots fault," Ciara told them. "The robot can only do what it is programmed to do."

"But, I put the instructions in myself," said Postman Pete. "They've been checked and double checked."

Sean laughed. "Yes. But, your right is the robot's left," Sean said.

The postmen looked puzzled.

"Stand facing opposite each other," Sean told them.

The postmen did as they were asked.

"Now walk to your left," Sean said.

The postmen walked in opposite directions. They both laughed.

"Now I understand what I did wrong," Postman Pete said. "Next time I will make sure I put the instructions in correctly."

Everybody laughed.

The End

Name: _____

• Write on the hands which is right and which is left.

• How do you remember which is your right hand and which is your left hand?

_____

Map

- Copy your map onto the grid below.
- Check that you have included all the places mentioned in the story.

- Compare your maps with other groups.
- Are they the same? _____

Instructions

Name: _____

- Write down your sequence of instructions below. Remember to put each instruction on a new line.
- Make a key for the abbreviations you have used.

Key

Instructions

- How can you improve your instructions?

_____

_____

_____

_____

_____

Robots Today

Name: _____

- Find and print images from the Internet of how robots are used in our society today.

- Explain how this robot is useful.

_____

_____

_____

Magic Carpet – teachers' notes

Learning Objective
To understand that ICT can be used to develop images.

Curriculum Links
Art

- Experiment with designs, shapes and colours
- Explore a range of media and materials, to create artworks
- Edit, change size and shape of digital creations.

Revelation Natural Art is a more sophisticated program then Paint. It is possible to use images that have been scanned into the computer, as well as photographs and ClipArt. Unlike Paint it allows the user to increase and decrease the size of the tools, such as the Brush tool. This will allow the user to make larger marks and cover the surface area of their pictures quicker.

Activity One – Using a Scanner

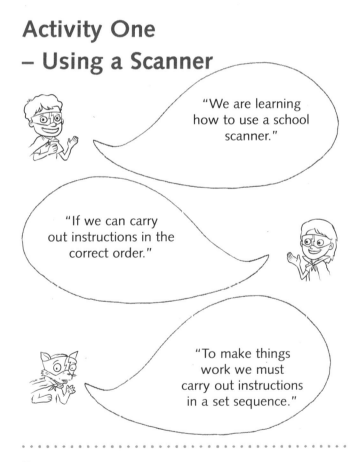

"We are learning how to use a school scanner."

"If we can carry out instructions in the correct order."

"To make things work we must carry out instructions in a set sequence."

Resources
- 'Magic Carpet' Story
- 'Using a Scanner' activity sheet
- Computers
- Digital projector
- Whiteboard
- Laptop
- Scanner
- Scanner software
- Image search engine.

Introduction

Familiarise yourself with the school's scanner and the software it uses, before the lesson begins.

Read the 'Magic Carpet' story to the class. Ask the children what trees are like in winter. Ask what Callum means by the words, "...everything is so bare..." Discuss the differences between evergreen trees and deciduous trees. Explain apple trees like the one Callum and Lucy went to see in Great Aunt Matilda's garden lose all their leaves in winter. Show the children some images using an image search engine of what apple trees look like in the Winter.

Draw a simple outline of a tree in winter on the Whiteboard. Point out that there are no leaves, fruit or blossoms.

Main Activity

Tell the children they are going to draw their own winter trees on the 'Using a Scanner' activity sheet. Explain they will scan their pictures into the computer using the school scanner. Demonstrate how to use the school's scanner software to preview their pictures. Show the children how to crop the page so the area to be scanned is only their picture and not the whole activity sheet.

Ask the children to save their scanned pictures with a name they will easily recognise in their My Documents folder. Explain they are going to use their picture again at a later date. Check each child has saved their picture of a tree in winter successfully.

After they have scanned their pictures and saved them, the children should write the instructions on how they scanned their image on the 'Using a Scanner' activity sheet. Explain that instructions have to be written in the correct order.

Plenary

Ask the children to swap their instructions with a partner. Ask them to check if their partner has remembered each step. Are the instructions in the correct order? Could they use their partner's instructions to scan their own pictures? Encourage the children to edit their instructions as necessary.

Extension

Ask the children to type their revised instructions in word. These can be printed and displayed near the computers and scanner for future reference.

Activity Two – Seasons

"We are learning how to save and edit our work using a graphics program."

Resources

- 'Magic Carpet' Story
- 'Seasons' activity sheet
- Saved picture of tree in winter from previous activity
- Computers
- Digital projector
- Whiteboard
- Laptop
- Scanner
- Image search engine.

Introduction

Before the lesson begins scan the 'Seasons' activity sheet into the computer to be used with a program such as Paint. Check the image search engine to ensure you are able to find pictures of trees during the different seasons before the lesson begins.

Read the 'Magic Carpet' story to the class. Ask the children what was the apple tree in Great Aunt Matilda's garden like in the spring. List some key words on the whiteboard such as leaves and blossom. What colour was the blossom? Tell the children it was pink just like the picture on the magic carpet and read the relevant part of the story that shows this:

"Callum and Lucy were amazed to see the apple tree was full of beautiful pink blossom, just like the picture on the magic carpet."

Show the children some images using an image search engine of what trees look like in the Spring. Ask the children what the apple tree was like in the summer and write down some of the key words on the whiteboard. Read the relevant part of the story to the children, which explains what the apple tree was like in the Summer:

"The carpet landed back in Great Aunt Matilda's garden under the big apple tree. But, this time the blossom had all gone. The tree was thick with luxurious, dark green leaves."

Show the children some images using an image search engine of what apple trees look like in the Summer. Repeat the same procedure for the tree in Autumn. Ask what the tree looked like and which part of the story gives them this information. Read the relevant part of the 'Magic Carpet' story to the children:

"He took his last photo of Great Aunt Matilda's apple tree, laden with apples. The leaves were beginning to turn golden brown and orange."

Show the children some images using an image search engine of what apple trees look like in the Autumn. Compare the differences between the trees during the different seasons. Ask them to look carefully at the different colours of the leaves throughout the seasons.

Main Activity

Explain to the children they are going to use their saved picture of a tree in winter and copy and paste their image onto the 'Seasons' activity sheet.

Ask the children to open their saved image of a tree in winter. Demonstrate how to copy the images using the right mouse button. Explain that the copy is the same as the original. Ask the children to paste the image into the first square of the activity sheet. Tell the children they will need to scale the image smaller to fit one of the squares on the 'Seasons' activity sheet. Demonstrate how to do this by moving the handles at the corners of the image.

When they are happy with the size of the tree they should save the activity sheet in their My Documents folder with a name they will easily recognise using the 'Save as' command. Tell the children to re-copy the re-sized image and paste it three times into each of the remaining squares of the 'Seasons' activity sheet. They should now re-save their work by clicking on save. Ensure the children understand the different functions of the 'save' and 'save as' commands.

Explain to the children they are going to change the trees to show how they change according to the different seasons. One of the trees can stay the same as it shows the tree in winter. They can use the pencil and brush tools to colour the other three trees to show spring, summer and autumn.

After creating their trees, ask the children to label each tree to illustrate which season it shows, using the Text tool to produce a text box and typing the name of the season into it. Remind them to save their work at regular intervals.

Plenary

Print the children's season pictures for display. Share the children's work and discuss how they have used the copy and paste tools to produce their tree in different seasons. Identify the original tree in each picture. Praise the children who have managed to produce four very different looking images, which identify the changes during the different seasons and have labelled them correctly.

Explain that the changes in the apple tree during the different seasons, is part of the life-cycle of the tree. Cut open an apple and show the children the seeds. Tell them if they plant these seeds they will be able to grow a new apple tree.

Extension

Plant some apple seeds in the classroom. Encourage the children to water them regularly and keep a record of the changes as they seedlings grow. Some of the seedlings will not survive but, point out that the strongest will eventually grow into apple trees.

Activity Three – Pointillism

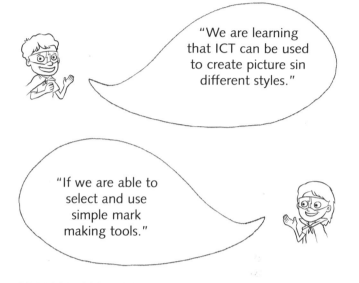

"We are learning that ICT can be used to create picture sin different styles."

"If we are able to select and use simple mark making tools."

Resources
- 'Magic Carpet' story
- 'Pointillism' activity sheet
- Computers
- Printer
- Digital projector
- Painting programs such as Revelation Natural Art
- Whiteboard
- Laptop
- Scanner
- Image search engine.

Introduction

Read the 'Magic Carpet' story to the children. Ask them what the picture on the carpet was. What season do trees have blossom on them? What happened to the carpet? How did they fix the carpet? What season did the picture on the carpet show when they had finished?

Look at the work of George Seurat. Discuss how he has used the pointillist technique to produce Courbevoie (1886) and The Morning Walk (1885). There are also some nice examples of trees in the pointillist style by Henri-Edmond Cross, which can be used to illustrate the desired outcome. In particular, Apres-midi a Paridigon (1907) and La Plagede Saint-Clair (1906-7). Both these artists' paintings can be found and enlarged on the whiteboard using an image search engine.

Explain to the children that Georges Seurat and Henri-Edmond Cross have not painted lines in these pictures. They have used small dots of colour and the eyes mix the colours together to create the image. Tell them using darker and lighter shades on different parts of the pictures can produce a 3D effect. Demonstrate the use of colours in the artists' paintings and show them how, when the pictures are viewed from a distance, the colours merge.

Tell the children they will be using ICT tools in a paint program to produce their own pointillist pictures of a tree just like the one in the 'Magic Carpet' story.

Main Activity

Load the 'Pointillism' activity sheet into Paint using a scanner. Show the children how to change the size to the largest Round Brush or Square Brush tool by selecting it with a left click. Demonstrate how to make dots on the screen by moving the mouse to the desired locations and clicking the left mouse button.

Show the children how to edit the colour palette in Paint by using the Edit colour option in the Colours tab on the menu bar. Demonstrate how to Define Custom Colours by clicking on the colour spectrum and moving the arrow up and down the saturation bar. When they have found the colour they like they should Add to Custom Colours and click OK.

However, Paint can be rather restrictive to use in that it is not possible to make the brush size any larger than the three settings available. This is where it must be beneficial if the school has another painting and drawing program available, such as Revelation Natural Art. This program allows the user to increase the brush size so the picture can be coloured in the pointillist style more easily.

Allow time for the children to experiment and develop their own pointillist tree pictures on the template of the 'Pointillism' activity sheet using their own custom colours. Show the children how to use the undo command to fix a mistake or mark they do not want.

Plenary

Print the children's work for display. If time permits the children could also compare the use of other mediums to create pictures in the pointillist style, such as pastels, felt pens or tissue paper. Share and discuss the pros and cons of using the computer to develop pictures in a

pointillist style. Encourage them to describe the effects produced. Is it easier or harder than other methods? Point out how the use of colour and the pointillist effect looks very impressive when viewed from a distance. Tell them if they make mistakes it is often easier to correct when they are using the computer.

Extension

As well as colouring the tree in a pointillist style some children may also be able to design and colour in the backgrounds of their tree pictures.

Activity Four – Storyboard

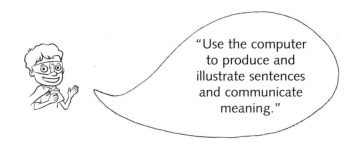

"Use the computer to produce and illustrate sentences and communicate meaning."

Resources

- 'Magic Carpet' story
- 'Storyboard' activity sheet
- Data projector
- Laptop
- Image search engine
- Drawing program like Paint
- Printer
- Computers.

Introduction

Read the story 'Magic Carpet' to the class. Ask the children to identify the beginning, middle and end of the story. Ask the children if they had a magic carpet, where they would want to go. List their ideas. Pick one idea and ask what sort of things would, they see there. List their suggestions. Demonstrate how these could be used to develop a story with a beginning, middle and an end.

Main Activity

Explain to the class they are going to write and illustrate their own 'Magic Carpet' stories. Encourage the children to draw their own images using a drawing program. They could print and paste these onto the 'Magic Carpet' story activity sheet or copy and paste them straight in, resizing them on the computer to fit in the storyboard.

Scan the 'Magic Carpet' story activity sheet into the computer and load into a program such as Paint. Tell the children they need to write some sentences to tell their story. This could be done by printing the sheets with their images on first or by adding text straight to the sheet on the computer depending on the ability and confidence of the individual child.

Plenary

Let the children read and show their stories to the class.

Extension

Ask the children to stick their 'Magic Carpet' stories into a class book which they can look at during library or reading time. Tell them to ensure their name is on their story so readers will know who the author is. Some children may also be able to design a front cover for the book using the computer.

Magic Carpet

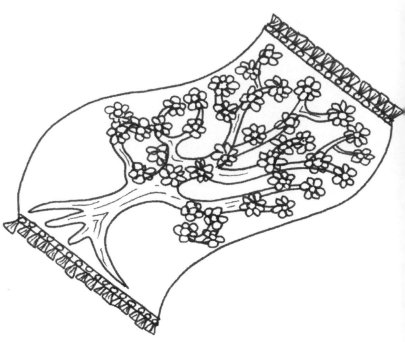

"I can't do this," Callum threw his homework book across the table.

Lucy sighed. "Yes. This homework's too hard."

"I don't even know what to do it on," Callum moaned. "How can Mrs White expect us to do homework on seasons when its winter and everything is so bare and cold?"

"I was thinking I might draw some pictures of Great Aunt Matilda's big apple tree. But, it's difficult to do it from memory."

"It would be easier if I could take photos," said Callum.

"Yes, or collect some samples. But, the homework has to be in tomorrow." Lucy said.

The doorbell rang.

Callum rushed to find out who it was. He was surprised to see the postman holding a strange, long, tube-like parcel.

Together they ripped off the brown paper to reveal a fantastic woollen carpet. On the carpet there was a big picture of a tree covered in beautiful pink blossom.

There was a note attached to the carpet. Callum read the note:

Dear Callum and Lucy,

This carpet will take you anywhere you want to go. It is a magic carpet. Love from

Great Aunt Matilda xxx

"Wow! A magic carpet! We could use it to see what Great Aunt Matilda's tree is like during the different seasons. I could take my camera," Callum said.

"But, that that would mean travelling through time," Lucy replied. "I don't think that's what Great Aunt Matilda meant. She probably meant travel to different countries and places, not through time."

"So?" Callum snapped back.

"I don't think it will work. It's impossible to travel through time," Lucy said.

"Well, we won't know if we don't try," Callum said.

Callum fetched his camera and Lucy got a bag. They took the carpet outside into the garden and sat on it with their legs crossed.

"How does it work?" Callum asked.

Lucy shrugged.

"I wish to go forward in time to see Great Aunt Matilda's apple tree in the Spring," she shouted.

The carpet wiggled. The carpet jiggled. Callum and Lucy held on tight. The carpet leapt into the air. It flew over the houses and whizzed along the familiar route to Great Aunt Matilda's house.
It landed in Great Aunt Matilda's garden. Callum and Lucy were amazed to see the apple tree was full of beautiful pink blossom, just like the picture on the magic carpet.

"It worked. It's spring," Callum said.

He quickly took some photos of the tree. Lucy picked some of the blossom and put it in her bag.

"What are you two doing here?" Great Aunt Matilda asked, making them both jump.

Lucy explained.

"But, you shouldn't use the carpet for time travel. If anything goes wrong you might not be able to get back home. It's very dangerous," Great Aunt Matilda warned them.

"Oh, I never thought of that," Lucy said. "Make sure you go straight back home to your own time," Great Aunt Matilda ordered. Lucy and Callum both agreed they would and Great Aunt Matilda went back indoors.

"That's the end of that then," Lucy said.

They sat cross-legged on the carpet. "I wish to go forward in time to see Great Aunt Matilda's apple tree in the Summer," Callum shouted.

Lucy gasped.

The carpet wiggled. The carpet jiggled. Callum and Lucy held on tight. The carpet leapt into the air. It flew straight up and up and then stopped. Then it began to whizz back down so fast, they thought they were going to leave their stomachs behind. The carpet landed back in Great Aunt Matilda's garden under the big apple tree. But, this time the blossom had all gone. The tree was thick with luxurious, dark green leaves.

Callum quickly took some more photos. Lucy picked a small branch of leaves and put it in her bag. When she turned around she saw Great Aunt Matilda racing down the garden path toward them.

"Quick we've got to go," Lucy yelled to Callum.

They both jumped onto the carpet.

"I wish to go forward in time to see Great Aunt Matilda's apple tree in the Autumn," they shouted together and laughed.

The carpet wiggled. The carpet jiggled. Callum and Lucy held on tight. The carpet leapt into the air. It flew straight up and up into the clouds. The clouds got thicker and darker. It started to rain. There was a massive crash and a bright flashing light. Ka-pow! The carpet was hit by lightening. The wool caught fire. Lucy and Callum tried to stamp out the flames. The carpet plummeted to ground. They clutched the sides. The carpet spun and it twirled and crashed right into Great Aunt Matilda's apple tree. Lucy and Callum were thrown on to the grass.

"Ouch!" Lucy cried.

Thump! Something hit Callum on the head.

"What's that?"

"It's an apple," Lucy said and put it in her bag. She looked at the carpet. "Oh no! The picture is all burnt. The blossom has all gone. It's ruined." She shook her head. "We should go home. Great Aunt Matilda was right, time travel is dangerous."

Callum nodded in agreement. He took his last photo of Great Aunt Matilda's apple tree, laden with apples. The leaves were beginning to turn golden brown and orange.

They both sat back on the carpet.

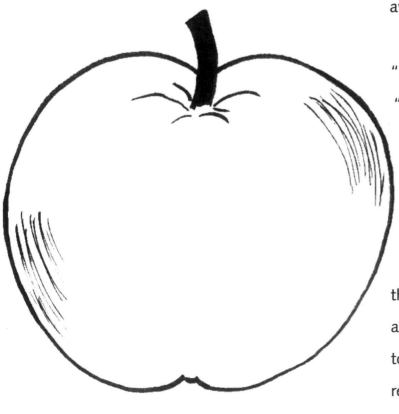

"I wish we were safe at home, back in our own time," Lucy shouted.

Nothing happened.

"What's wrong?" Callum asked.

Lucy shrugged. "I think the magic carpet is broken."

"How are we going to get back to own time?" Callum groaned.

Great Aunt Matilda was rushing down the garden path toward them. They couldn't get away. The carpet wouldn't move.

"I told you so," Great Aunt Matilda said. "You're going to have to fix the holes yourselves." She handed them some carpet hooks and wool.

Callum and Lucy used the carpet hooks to weave more wool into the carpet to replace the blossom pattern that had been burnt away. They hooked the wool into the carpet to make the tree thick with leaves and bright red, shiny apples. It took ages. Both Lucy and

Callum had blisters on their fingers where they worked so hard. When they had finished they said goodbye to Great Aunt Matilda and sat back on the carpet.

"I wish we were safe at home, back in our own time," Lucy whispered.

The carpet wiggled. The carpet jiggled. Callum and Lucy held on tight. The carpet leapt into the air. It flew over the houses and whizzed along the familiar route back home to their own garden. Callum and Lucy had never been so happy to see the trees so bare. Callum took a photo. Lucy picked a twig up from the grass and put it in her bag.

"All I have to do now is print off my pictures and I've finished the homework," Callum said.

"I don't think we will use the carpet again though," Lucy said. "It's far too dangerous."

"I don't know," replied Callum. "I think we could use it, just not for time travel."

Lucy grinned.

The End

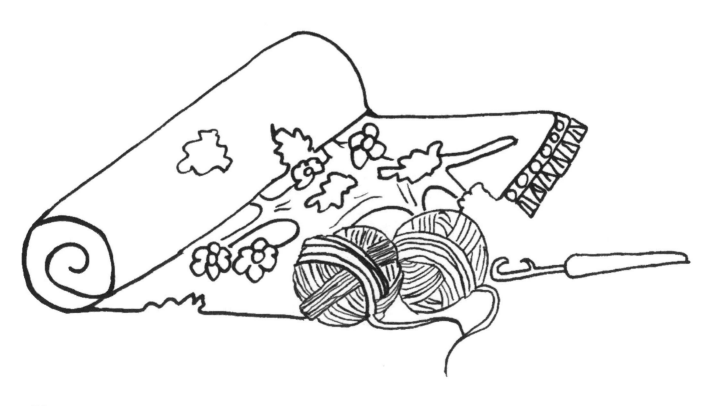

Name: _____

- Draw a picture of an apple tree in winter.

- Scan your picture into the computer and save a copy.
- Write instructions on how you scanned the picture.

_____

_____

_____

_____

_____

Seasons

Name: _____

- Copy and paste your picture of an apple tree in winter into each box.

- Write the season below each tree.

*Using stories to teach **ICT** Ages 6-7*

Name: _____

- Use the computer to colour the picture of the tree.

- What season is your tree?

Storyboard

Name: _____

- Imagine you find a magic carpet and it will fly anywhere you want it to go.
  Where will you go? What do you see when you get there?
  What is the weather like?
- Write and draw your own magic carpet story.

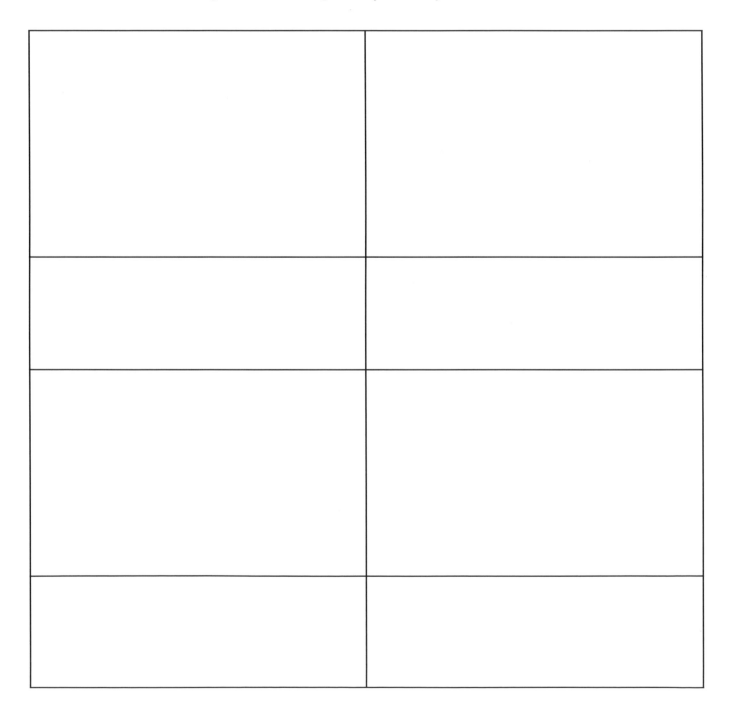

The Ice Cream Parlour Break-in – teachers' notes

Learning Objective
To develop an understanding of similarity and difference by asking questions, which can be answered with a 'yes' or 'no' response.

Curriculum Links
Mathematics

- Make sense of data in an increasingly digital world
- Generate and explore questions that require the collection and analysis of information
- Use simple branching databases to find out the answers to specific questions
- Collect, group, match, sort and represent information for a purpose and store it using ICT.

Science

- Discover humans are similar to each other in some ways and different in others
- Explore human variation making observation and comparisons
- Recognise some differences between themselves and other children can be measured.

Activity One – Wanted

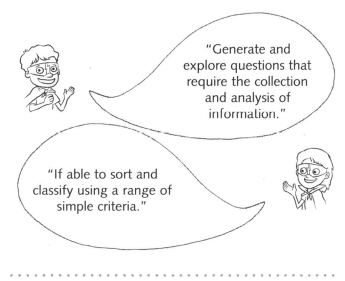

"Generate and explore questions that require the collection and analysis of information."

"If able to sort and classify using a range of simple criteria."

Resources
- 'Ice Cream Parlour Break-in' story
- 'Wanted' activity sheet
- Computers
- Printer
- Digital projector
- Whiteboard
- Laptop.

Introduction

Before you read the story to the class, ask the children what vandalism is. Have they ever seen anything that has been vandalised? Talk about examples of vandalism in the local area that may have affected them. Tell them graffiti is a form of vandalism and if someone breaks the play equipment at the park on purpose this is also vandalism. Ask the children how does seeing things broken and ruined in this way make them feel.

Read the 'Ice Cream Parlour Break-in' story to the class. Ask the children how they would feel if they were Mr Robbins, the owner of the Ice Cream parlour.

Main Activity

Explain humans are similar to each other in some ways and different in others. We have different colour hair and different colour eyes and we are different heights. All these things can be used to help identify people. Ask the children what distinguishing features did the eye witnesses identify in the person who vandalised the ice cream parlour. Read the relevant parts of the story to remind them:

- "He had dark hair, green eyes and rather big ears." Mr Robbins
- "He was small with short, dark hair. I only saw him from the back, but noticed he was wearing blue jeans and white trainers." Ben
- "The kid was short and scrawny, with green eyes and freckles. He must have been about ten years old." Jerry

Tell the children they are going to make a 'Wanted' poster of Billy. Read the story again and ask the children to make notes of the suspect's description. They should use these notes to make their own photo-fit picture of what Billy looks like, using a program such as: www.myavatareditor.com

Demonstrate how to use the program by making an avatar of yourself. When they have made their photo-fit picture they can save as an Export jpg to their own documents and print them out. Ask them to stick their pictures on the 'Wanted' activity sheet, as a record of their achievements. Encourage them to write a detailed description in the space provided on the 'Wanted' activity sheet.

Plenary

Discuss with the children how they could change the way they look and whether they would still be recognised. How did Billy try to disguise his appearance? Remind the children that some physical differences between people are permanent, such as eye colour and some can be changed, such as the length of their hair.

Extension

In small groups, the children should discuss how Mr Robbins could deter anyone breaking into the Ice Cream parlour again. Encourage them to think of technological ideas like security cameras and burglar alarms. How would these have helped?

Activity Two – Questions

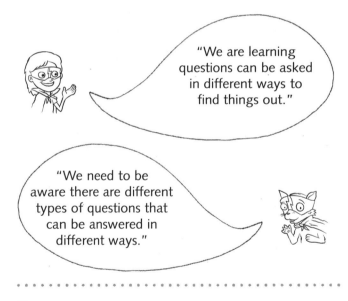

"We are learning questions can be asked in different ways to find things out."

"We need to be aware there are different types of questions that can be answered in different ways."

Resources
- 'Ice Cream Parlour Break-in' story
- 'Questions' activity sheet
- Digital photographs of the children in the class.

Introduction

Read the 'Ice Cream Parlour Break-in' story to the class. Tell the children there are different types of questions that can be answered in different ways. Explain open ended questions can have any answer. Where as, closed questions are normally short specific one word answers like yes or no. Explain a rhetorical question is one where no answer is expected.

Explain to the class they are going to be concentrating on questions that they can answer yes or no to. Play the 'Who Am I?' game where one child pretends they are a character from a book, TV, movie, or historical figure, sports celebrity, etc and the rest of the class have to guess who it is by asking 'yes' or 'no' questions. The main focus of these activities is to develop and practice questioning techniques. Ensure the children understand the difference between questions and answers.

Main Activity

Reread the 'Ice Cream Parlour Break-in' story. Ask the children to list any questions that are in the story. Ask them to identify if these questions are opened, closed questions or rhetorical questions. Give the children a copy of the 'Questions' activity sheet.

Here is a list of all the questions and answers:

- What has happened here? Open
- Can you think of anyone who might have wanted to vandalise the ice cream parlour? Open
- What did this boy look like? Open
- Have you found the person who broke into the ice cream parlour yet? Closed
- How do you know about the break in? Open
- How could I deliver newspapers covered in footprints? Open
- What did he look like? Open
- Did you see where he went? Closed
- Is there anyone here? Closed
- Is Mrs Walls, the shop owner around? Closed
- Do you know when she will be back? Closed
- Are you a relative? Closed
- What are you doing here? Open
- Your son? Rhetorical
- Who is the girl with the green eyes and the long blond curls? Open
- A girl? Rhetorical
- Billy, where are you? Open
- Why are you wearing that blond wig, Billy? Open
- Are you the one who vandalised the ice cream parlour? Closed
- Why did you do it? Open.

Plenary

Go through the answers as a class and ask how they came to their decisions. Explain recognising and using closed questions that can be answered with a 'yes' or 'no' response is important when using and making branching databases.

Extension

Ask the children to play a 'Guess Who' type game using digitally produced photos of the class to find which person has been chosen. Use photos of four girls and four boys that are distinctively different in some way, or they could use the characters in the branching database activity sheet.

Activity Three – Branching Database

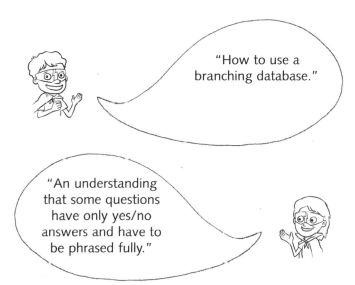

"How to use a branching database."

"An understanding that some questions have only yes/no answers and have to be phrased fully."

Resources
- 'Ice Cream Parlour Break-in' story
- 'Branching Database' activity sheet
- Computers
- Printer
- Digital projector
- Whiteboard
- Laptop
- www.mape.org.uk/activities/sorting_games/index.htm
- Branching database program such as Decisions 3 or Flexitree 2.

Decisions 3 is a simple-to-use branching database in which information can be entered in the form of a 'decision tree'. The program has been designed to be as easy to use as possible and can be used by pupils from the age of six years upwards. Flexitree 2 is a similar program that enables the user to create and edit branching data bases. It is also possible to view the whole 'decision tree'.

Introduction

Read the 'Ice Cream Parlour Break-in' story to the class.

Tell the children a branching database is a way of classifying a group of objects and identifying specific person or item by asking a series of 'yes' or 'no' questions. Explain PC Baskin planned to use the description of the person who vandalised the ice cream parlour in a similar database at the police station.

It is advisable that before using a computer branching database children have the opportunity for lots of practice in physically describing and sorting objects. To begin, use a limited number of objects and only one thing to sort, such as colour or shape. The number of objects and criteria can gradually increase to build up the database.

Main Activity

Show the children the 'Branching Database' activity sheet. Look at each of the characters. Ask the children to look at the similarities and differences in the different characters. Ask them to list some questions that they can answer 'yes' or 'no' to, such as:

- Is it a boy?
- Does the person have short hair?
- Are they wearing glasses?
- Do they have a hat on?
- Are they tall?

Demonstrate using a tree diagram similar to the one on the following page. In this way, you can show the children on an interactive whiteboard one possible way how the eight characters can be sorted into the individual boxes below. Tell them they can use different questions to sort them in other ways as well.

Encourage the children to draw their own branching database to keep a record of their questions. This helps to ensure the questions asked have both a 'yes' and a 'no' answer.

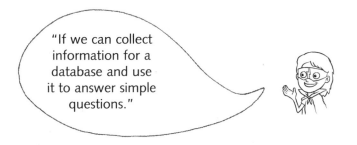

Branching database diagram

```
                    Is it
                   a boy?
        Yes  ←                  →  No

   Is the                          Does the girl have
   boy short?                      long hair?
 Yes ←        → No            Yes ←           → No

Does the boy   Does the boy    Does the girl    Does the girl
have freckles? have a hat?     have freckles?   have glasses?
Yes ↓   No ↓   Yes ↓   No ↓    Yes ↓    No ↓    Yes ↓    No ↓
```

Demonstrate how to input their questions into the software available and produce a branching database, which other people can also use to select one of the characters.

Plenary

Reinforce that a branching database can be used to classify and sort a wide range of things, such as fruit and vegetables, musical instruments, vehicles, materials, shapes, etc. Point out using the characters on the Branching database activity sheet is dependent on visual clues but, they can also use other senses to help sort things such as sounds, smell, taste and how things feel to touch.

Extension

The children can extend their skills and practice using a wide variety of branching databases online, using websites such as, www.mape.org.uk/activities/sorting_games/index.htm

Activity Four – Graphs

"If we can collect information for a database and use it to answer simple questions."

Resources

- 'Ice Cream Parlour Break-in' story
- 'Graphs' activity sheet
- Computers
- Printer
- Digital projector
- Whiteboard
- Laptop
- Graphic program or Word.

Introduction

Read the 'Ice Cream Parlour Break-in' story to the class. What colour eyes did the suspect have? How did this information help PC Baskin find out who committed the crime?

Explain to the children they are going to use a simple graphing program to record the eye colour of children in the class and create bar charts. Tell the children their data can be organised across the page in rows or in columns, whatever they prefer. Demonstrate how to enter the data into the table. This could be produced using the table facility in Word, if no other software is available in school. Demonstrate how to make a tally of the different eye colours in the class on the whiteboard. Ask the children to make a copy of this tally on the 'Graphs' activity sheet.

Explain that most data can be collected and presented as a bar chart. Tell the children this makes it easier to recognise quantities and see differences at a glance. Explain ICT is an excellent medium for creating bar charts.

Main Activity

Split the class into pairs. Talk about the software program they will be using and answer any questions. Remind the children about taking turns. Explain one person can input the data whilst the other checks the data is correct and then they can swap roles. Use the activity sheet 'Graphs' to make a draft copy of the work that will be input onto the computer.

Suggest the children label the rows or columns and give their graph a title. Encourage them to check they have got the numbers correct and have not missed any out.

Plenary

Ask the children to write a few sentences to explain what their graph shows. Encourage the children to share their sentences by reading them to the class. Tell them that even though the bars may be in different orders going vertically or horizontally across the page the actual information they show is the same.

Discuss the advantages of using ICT to produce graphs and charts. Explain to the children it is easier to see the information at a glance, questions can be answered more easily and it can be quicker.

Extension

Ask the children to produce graphs for other things that can be used to compare differences in themselves, such as:

- Hair colour
- Hair styles
- Shoe size
- Hand span
- Height.

Discuss how some things about their appearance can be changed and some can't.

The Ice Cream Parlour Break-in • • • • •

PC Baskin arrived at the ice cream parlour and was shocked to see the mess. There was ice cream everywhere. Caramel crunch and orange sherbet ice cream splattered the walls, raspberry ripple and pistachio ice cream plastered the floor and the coffee and blueberry flavours were splashed all over the windows.

"What has happened here?" he asked Mr Robbins.

Mr Robbins shook his head. "I arrived this morning to find the door had been broken and the shop vandalised. Who could have done such a thing?"

"Don't worry," PC Baskin reassured Mr Robbins. "I'll find out who did it. Can you think of anyone who might have wanted to vandalise the ice cream parlour?"

Mr Robbins shook his head again. "No one would want to wreck the ice cream parlour. Everyone loves ice cream. The children will be very disappointed when I don't have their favourite flavours to offer them. Yesterday, one boy got so upset when I ran out of

double chocolate chip he threw his money at me and ran out of the shop screaming."

"What did this boy look like?" PC Baskin asked.

"He had dark hair, green eyes and rather big ears," Mr Robbins said.

PC Baskin wrote the description down in his notebook. He was on his way back to the police station when he noticed some raspberry ripple footprints on the pavement outside the ice cream parlour. He followed the footprints along the street. At the corner he met Ben the milkman on his way home after finishing his morning deliveries.

"Hello PC Baskin," Ben the milkman said. "Have you found the person who broke into the ice cream parlour yet?"

"No, Ben! Not yet! How do you know about the break in?"

"I went past on my rounds at six o'clock this morning and the shop was fine. Everything was quiet. But, on my way back, the alarm was going off and the door was opened and I noticed the ice cream splashed all over the windows. I saw someone running away. He was small with short, dark hair. I only saw him from the back, but noticed he was wearing blue jeans and white trainers." Ben the milkman said.

PC Baskin wrote the description down in his notebook. "Thank you Ben this is very helpful. I can get some posters made to help find this boy to bring him in for questioning."

PC Baskin waved goodbye to Ben the milkman and continued to follow the raspberry ripple ice cream footsteps. The footsteps got fainter and fainter. Soon it was hard to see them at all. PC Baskin peered down at the pavement. He was concentrating so hard he walked right into a boy with short dark hair outside the newsagents. But, this boy was not small. He was very tall. It was Jerry, the paperboy.

"Careful!" Jerry the paperboy yelled. "You're the second person who has bumped into me today."

"I'm sorry Jerry," PC Baskin said. "I'm looking for the vandal who broke into the ice cream parlour this morning and didn't see you there. I've followed the raspberry ripple footprints this far and now they've disappeared."

"I'm not surprised they've disappeared," Jerry the paperboy said. "When I came out the newsagent this morning, a kid ran straight into me and knocked my trolley over, spilling all my newspapers and magazines onto the pavement. He left raspberry coloured footprints all over them. I was very cross. How could I deliver newspapers covered in footprints? They were ruined."

"What did he look like?" PC Baskin asked.

"The kid was short and scrawny, with green eyes and freckles. He must have been about ten years old."

PC Baskin wrote the description down in his notebook. "Did you see where he went?"

"He was very rude and yelled at me before running away. I think he went into the fancy dress shop, but that was hours ago."

PC Baskin thanked Jerry the paperboy for his help and headed toward the fancy dress shop. He was surprised to find nobody in the shop.

"Is there anyone here?" he called out.

"Hello, I'm Bella," a small girl said appearing from behind the counter. She had long blond curls and a very high-pitched voice.

"Oh, I didn't see you there," PC Baskin said. "Is Mrs Walls, the shop owner around?"

"No," Bella said in her high-pitched voice.

"Do you know when she will be back?"

"No," Bella said again.

PC Baskin could not help noticing that Bella had very green eyes and freckles. "Are you a relative?"

"Yes," Bella said.

At that moment Mrs Walls came rushing in. "Billy, I'm back," she called. She stopped abruptly when she saw the policeman. "Oh hello, PC Baskin what are you doing here?"

"Ah, good morning Mrs Walls, I'm investigating a break in at the ice cream parlour and a suspect was last seen entering the fancy dress shop."

"There's nobody here but, me and my son Billy," Mrs Walls said.

"Your son? Then who is the girl with the green eyes and the long blond curls?"

Mrs Walls looked puzzled. "A girl?"

"Yes. She must be about ten years old," PC Baskin told her.

They both looked around the shop but, nobody was there. The girl had vanished.

"Billy, where are you? Come here right now," Mrs Walls shouted.

Bella stood up from behind the counter.

Mrs Walls gasped. "Why are you wearing that blond wig, Billy?" she asked. "Take it off immediately."

Billy removed the wig to reveal his short dark hair and rather big ears. PC Baskin checked his notebook. This boy matched the eyewitness descriptions perfectly now he had taken the wig off.

"Are you the one who vandalised the ice cream parlour?" Mrs Walls asked her son.

"Yes," Billy whispered.

"Why did you do it?" Mrs Walls said.

Billy bowed his head. "I went to get my money back and when I couldn't find it, I lost my temper."

Mrs Walls and PC Baskin marched Billy to the ice cream parlour straight away to apologise to Mr Robbins. His punishment was to help clean up the mess and go everyday after school to help clean up for the next two months. Billy promised he would never do anything that silly ever again.

The End

Name: _____

- Make a photo-fit of Billy using the description in the story.

WANTED

FOR ICE CREAM PARLOUR BREAK-IN

- Description:

_____
_____
_____
_____

Questions

Name: _____

- Write the questions from the story below.
- Add whether the question is a closed, open or rhetorical question?

- Write your own closed question.

_____

_____

- Write your own open question.

_____

_____

Branching Database

Name: _____

- Use these characters to help you create a branching database.

- Add some more characters of your own.

Graphs

Name: _____

- Complete the tally chart of eye colour in your class.

Eye colour	Tally	Total
Green		
Brown		
Blue		
Grey		
Hazel		

- Use the information to make a block graph.

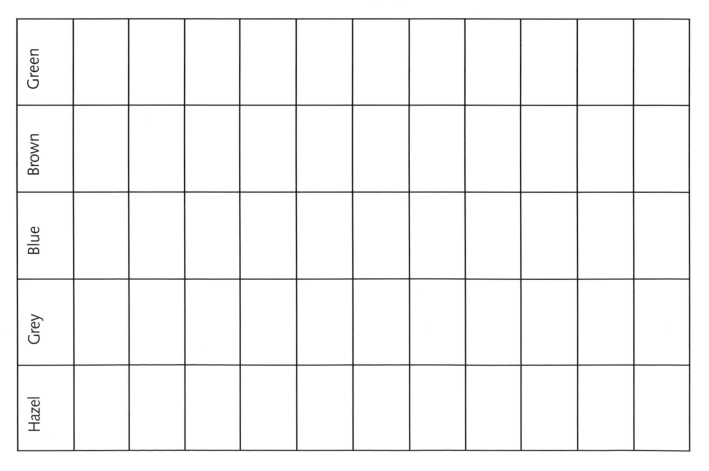

- Put this information onto the computer.

- Save and print your graphs.

Notes